Uganda

Ian Leggett

Oxfam **Fountain Publishers**

First published in 2001:

In Uganda, for East and Central Africa, by
  Fountain Publishers Ltd, Fountain House,
  Plot 55 Nkrumah Road, PO Box 488,
  Kampala, Uganda
  Tel: +256 41 259163/251112
  Fax: +256 41 251160/534973
  Email: fountain@starcom.co.ug
  http://www.fountainpublishers.com

In the rest of the world by
  Oxfam GB, 274 Banbury Road, Oxford OX2 7DZ, UK
  Tel: +44 (0)1865 311311
  Fax: +44 (0)1865 312600
  Email: publish@oxfam.org.uk
  http://www.oxfam.org.uk/publications

Distributed in the USA exclusively by
  Stylus Publishing LLC, PO Box 605,
  Herndon, VA 20172-0605, USA
  Tel: +1 (0)703 661 1581
  Fax: +1 (0)703 661 1547
  Email: styluspub@aol.com
  http://www.styluspub.com

Reprinted by Oxfam GB in 2004 (twice), 2005, 2006

© Oxfam GB 2001

ISBN 0 85598 454 6 (Oxfam GB)

ISBN 9970 02 270 9 (Fountain Publishers)

A catalogue record for this publication is available from the British Library.

Printed by
  Information Press, Eynsham

Published simultaneously by
  Oxfam GB in the UK and Fountain Publishers in Uganda

Series designed by
  Richard Morris, Stonesfield Design
  Typeset in Scala and Gill Sans.

Oxfam GB is a registered charity, no. 202 918, and is a member of Oxfam International.

Contents

Geoff Sayer

Contents

Geoff Sayer

Introduction: the creation of a state

Uganda is a young country. The announcement of its creation and of its status as a British protectorate was published in the London Gazette in 1894. Unfortunately, most of the people who lived in the territory that was described to the world as being Uganda had never heard of the London Gazette, nor did a country called Uganda mean anything to them. Not surprisingly they felt no allegiance to an imperial creation whose borders cut across existing economic, political, and social relationships.

The formation of Uganda was not the result of a gradual process of national integration. On the contrary, both its existence and its borders were determined almost entirely by competition between the imperial powers – Great Britain, Germany, and France – for control of territory in Africa and, specifically, for control of the head-waters of the River Nile.

Nevertheless, when Uganda was given its independence in 1962, there was a sense of optimism in the air. Unlike in Kenya, Uganda's neighbour to the east, the independence campaign in Uganda was not characterised by insurgency, violence, or bloodshed, and the transition to independence was orderly and relatively harmonious. Investments in education, health care, and in the creation of effective public services also help to explain the positive expectations that accompanied the achievement of independence.

▶ *Tumbling waters of the Nile at Bujagali Falls*

◀ *Sarah Aromorac walks beneath posters urging Ugandans to vote in the national referendum on 29 June 2000.*

Geoff Sayer

Uganda in turmoil and transformation

Yet within three years, rumours of plots and assassination attempts had become common currency. In 1966 the Prime Minister, Milton Obote, unilaterally suspended the constitution, the army destroyed the Kabaka's (king's) palace, and the President himself fled the country. During the next two decades, Uganda became notorious. Tyranny and oppression; corruption, black-marketeering, and economic collapse; tribalism, violation of human rights, and civil war – these were the epithets by which Uganda became known. Once described by Winston Churchill as the 'Pearl of Africa', after just 20 years of independence Uganda was widely seen as the basket case of the continent.

By 1985, Uganda appeared to be on the verge of fragmentation, with different armed factions controlling different parts of Kampala or areas of the country. The economy too was in a state of siege. It became increasingly difficult to do any kind of trade, either within Uganda or with the outside world. There was a desperate shortage of essential goods such as sugar, soap, and salt; inflation was rampant, smuggling was common, and the salaries paid to public servants had become worthless – literally a few pounds a month.

The situation began to change in 1986 when the National Resistance Army – the armed wing of the National Resistance Movement (NRM) – captured Kampala. A new government was installed, promising fundamental change. Under that government, which is still in power, Uganda is once again being heralded as a model in Africa.

▼ *A busy market at Kibuye on the outskirts of Kampala*

Geoff Sayer

▲ *Rush hour in Kampala*

▼ *Collecting clean water at Kaburere displaced camp, Kyondo subcounty, western Uganda*

In 1987 the government introduced an economic recovery programme which is widely perceived to have been both ambitious and successful. Inflation was over 200 per cent in 1986–7, but had dropped to 4 per cent in 2000. Growth rates have been consistently positive for more than a decade, making Uganda's economic performance one of the most successful in Africa.

There has been an impressive transformation of Uganda's commercial, economic, and social infrastructure. Pot-holed roads have largely been repaired, the phone system has been modernised, and Kampala is now a thriving, busy city. Just as important for Uganda's citizens has been the rehabilitation of the country's public services, epitomised by the creation of an increasingly visible and credible local government. But the most dramatic change has been in education, with the introduction of Universal Primary Education (UPE), and a root and branch transformation of university level education.

Obstacles to development – conflict and inequality

It is not surprising that foreign donors, international financial institutions, and the government itself talk of a 'dramatic turnaround', and of Uganda being 'an inspirational success story'. But economic growth does not mean that all Ugandans have benefited from current policies. There has been a growth in inequality, and an increasingly common feeling that some people and some parts of the country are doing very nicely, while others are being left behind.

The progress of the last 15 years is all the more remarkable given the circumstances in which it has been made. Most serious has been the scale of ongoing internal conflict, especially in parts of northern and western Uganda where there is chronic insecurity, resulting in social dislocation and economic underdevelopment in the areas most affected. In addition, there is a high financial cost to the nation as a whole because of the need to maintain high levels of military supervision and because of the 'lost' revenue that could have been contributed to the national economy if peace had prevailed.

► Carrying a heavy jerrycan of water home. In Kyondo sub-county, where this boy lives, more than 13,000 people have remained displaced since 1997, following rebel attacks. The United Nations has estimated that there are more than 600,000 internally displaced people in Uganda.

▼ Danish International Development Assistance (DANIDA) is just one of the foreign donors providing aid to Uganda. DANIDA's EARS programme works with disabled Ugandans to provide education and training.

Conflict has had an external dimension, too. Military action in Rwanda, Congo, and Sudan has brought Uganda into the centre of complex regional conflicts. These involvements seem to have done little to enhance life and security, have left Uganda's leadership exposed to criticism, and have generally detracted from its reputation as a model of new leadership.

As in many other African countries, the increase in prevalence of HIV and AIDS has had huge impacts on individual, household, and national well-being in Uganda. Because HIV/AIDS primarily affects the economically productive population (those aged between 15 and 50), the illness can spell poverty and destitution for individuals and families, as well as a loss of wealth to the national economy.

Another obstacle has been limited room for manoeuvre in terms of economic development. For decades, Uganda has been dependent for its foreign exchange (and thus its ability to trade with the world beyond its borders) on the export of agricultural products such as coffee and tobacco. The perpetuation of an economy that has such a narrow base represents a constraint on growth of profound proportions. The structure of an economy, however, cannot be changed quickly and the government has relied on aid and debt relief to generate the resources needed to finance the cost of its rehabilitation and modernisation programme.

Whilst the Uganda government has pursued an economic policy that conforms to priorities and thinking within the World Bank and its major donors, it has taken a much more independent line in terms of political development, and has resisted the notion that a multi-party system based on a 'western' model is necessarily part of democracy. Arguing that a multi-party system has been a key part of Uganda's past problems, the NRM's alternative has been to govern through a no-party, movement-based system. Although it has opponents and critics from within Uganda and externally, the 'Movement model' continues to be popular with, and endorsed by, the people of Uganda as a whole.

The collective endorsement of the NRM, however, hides deep divisions between its supporters and others. These divisions lie along well-established social and economic fault lines. The people who live in southern and western Uganda are wealthier, have access to better public services, enjoy greater levels of personal security, and, for all these reasons, tend to support the Movement and the status quo. On the other hand, those who live in the north suffer conflict and violence to varying degrees, are poorer, and have less access to public services which are, in any case, of poorer quality. Many of these people reject the NRM, and those policies and practices of government that have left them feeling excluded and unprotected.

Because the contrasts within Uganda are no more severe than in many other countries in Africa, and because they do not pose a fundamental threat to national security, there is perhaps a tendency to accept them as an inevitable part of 'life'. But the NRM came to power promising something better, not more of the same. It is this value base which has made the NRM different, and which explains why it continues to arouse strong feelings among Ugandans, either of support or of opposition. Ultimately, the NRM will be judged by the principles and commitments it has laid down for itself. Irrespective of the verdict, if that judgement is made peacefully and openly, that in itself will be a milestone in Uganda's history.

▼ *Poor rains have reduced crop and milk yields in northern Uganda, forcing families to seek other employment. Lokol Nakong and her daughter Otiang Napeyok are breaking stones into gravel, which is bought by local builders. This is hard work – it takes five or six hours to fill a single can. For the price of a can the women can buy just 2kg of maize meal.*

Geoff Sayer

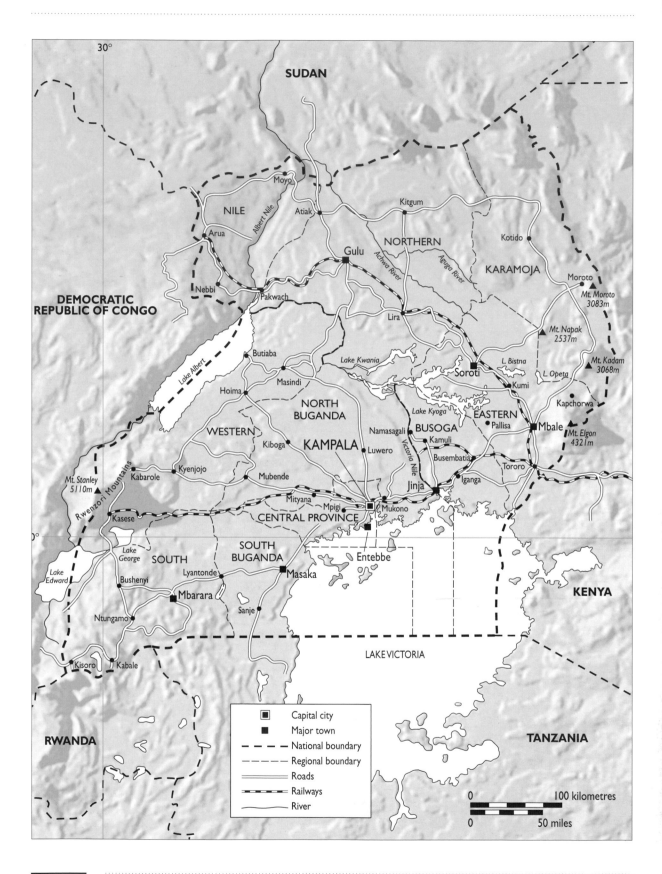

SUDAN

NILE

Moyo

Atiak

Kitgum

NORTHERN

Kotido

Arua

Albert Nile

Gulu

Achwa River

Aguga River

KARAMOJA

Moroto

Mt. Moroto
3083m

DEMOCRATIC
REPUBLIC OF CONGO

Nebbi

Pakwach

Lira

Mt. Napak
2537m

Butiaba

Lake Kwania

Soroti

L. Bistna

Mt. Kadam
3068m

Lake Albert

Hoima

Masindi

NORTH
BUGANDA

Lake Kyoga

Kumi

L. Opeta

Kapchorwa

WESTERN

Kiboga

KAMPALA

Luwero

Namasagali

BUSOGA

Kamuli

EASTERN

Pallisa

Mbale

Mt. Elgon
4321m

Mt. Stanley
5110m

Rwenzori Mountains

Kabarole

Kyenjojo

Mubende

Mityana

Mpigi

Mukono

Busembatia

Iganga

Jinja

Tororo

Victoria Nile

CENTRAL PROVINCE

Kasese

Lake
George

SOUTH

Lake
Edward

Bushenyi

Lyantonde

SOUTH
BUGANDA

Entebbe

Masaka

KENYA

Mbarara

Sanje

Ntungamo

Kisoro

Kabale

LAKE VICTORIA

RWANDA

TANZANIA

Capital city

Major town

National boundary

Regional boundary

Roads

Railways

River

0   100 kilometres

0   50 miles

30°

0°

The country and its people

Uganda is a relatively small country, about the size of the United Kingdom, and with a population of approximately 22 million. Over 80 per cent of Ugandan people live in villages and small trading centres. Uganda has only one city, the capital, Kampala.

Despite its small area, Uganda encompasses remarkable physical and biological diversity. This diversity is a consequence of the fact that the heat and humidity associated with equatorial Africa – the equator lies just a few miles to the south of Kampala – are modified by Uganda's altitude and its distance from the sea. Although Uganda is a land-locked country with no coastline, around 20 per cent of the country consists of lakes – the largest and best-known being Lake Victoria. These lakes help to moderate the equatorial climate and also explain why Uganda, located hundreds of miles from the nearest ocean, exports millions of pounds-worth of fish each year.

Much of Uganda is a plateau, approximately 1000m above sea level. To the east, near the border with Kenya, are free-standing volcanic mountains such as Mount Elgon, Mount Moroto, and Mount Napak, where equatorial mountain forests survive in sharp contrast to the vast and semi-arid plains that stretch northwards to Sudan. The western borders are even more spectacular, with the high and rugged peaks of the Rwenzori Mountains towering over glaciers and snowfields and, at low altitudes, dense forests.

The most important physical feature of the country is the River Nile. For many centuries, long before European powers defined Uganda as being strategically important because of its identification as the source of the Nile, the river was a natural meeting point for different political systems, ecological zones, and ethnic groups.

▼ *Jackson fills his basket with Nile perch bought at Lake Victoria. Jackson has built up his own business over the last ten years, cycling huge distances to buy fish from Lake Victoria and Lake Kijanebarorato. He can carry a load of 130 kg of fish on his bicycle, Uganda's essential small business vehicle.*

Geoff Sayer

PAPYRUS: THE REED OF THE NILE

Papyrus became the most important writing material in the ancient world, and the word 'paper' is derived from it. It was first produced by the Egyptians more than 5000 years ago, from papyrus reeds harvested on the banks of the Nile. Today, the papyrus plant is almost extinct in Egypt, but continues to flourish in Uganda, in the marshes of the Nile and the broad valleys that run into Lake Victoria and Lake Kyoga.

Just six kilometres from Kampala city centre, Sipriano Byaruhanga has been making a business out of papyrus for the last ten years. 'For me, papyrus was a last resort. After I completed primary school, I was employed as a teacher. But after ten years I lost my job, when the government insisted on all teachers being qualified. So I had to leave my family and come here, to cut papyrus. I go back to visit my wife and children every three months or so.'

Sipriano is cutting the tall, leafless stems with a machete, lopping off the tassel-head before lying the papyrus out to dry. The taller papyrus found deep in the swamp is best for Sipriano's use. 'Sometimes I go far into the swamp. It can be dangerous in the rainy season, if a strong current comes. That's why I always carry this stick. There are deep places.' The papyrus roots form a thick sedge above the water, supporting his weight. Crickets buzz and unseen birds chatter. Uganda is unrivalled in Africa for the diversity of its birds, with well over 1000 species recorded. The papyrus gonolek and papyrus canary are among those which can only be seen in the swamps – though with difficulty.

'After cutting, I leave the papyrus for two or three weeks to dry before I carry it home,' Sipriano continues. 'I make it up into mats and sell them for house roofing, or floor mats. It can also be used for fencing. It's cheaper than grass for roofs, and easier to find around here. The price is 500 shillings [20p] each. I stitch them together with string. It's the cutting that takes the time. I can make ten mats from a day's cutting.'

Uganda's fertile crescent...

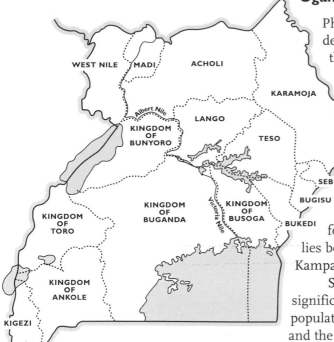

Physical features and the climate are the principal determinants of the most important element of the country's economy, agriculture. By and large, the soils of Uganda to the south and west of the River Nile are fertile and well watered. These lands – lying between the Kenyan border to the east, Mount Elgon, the River Nile, and Lake Kyoga to the north, and the spectacular Rift Valley to the west – form a fertile and productive crescent. In the past, luxuriant equatorial forests clothed much of this land. The remnants of these are to be found in isolated forests such as Mabira, which lies between Uganda's two biggest urban centres, Kampala and Jinja.

Such an environment provided the conditions for significant agricultural development, a relatively dense population, and, consequently, the division of labour and the creation of relatively complex patterns of production and consumption. The result was the emergence of a number of kingdoms with hierarchical structures, in which chiefs were appointed by a king, peasant farmers were required to offer part of their agricultural production as tribute, and military force was used to secure or enforce territorial expansion. These kingdoms, particularly Buganda, played a critically important role in the history of the colonisation of Uganda as well as in the political and economic development of independent Uganda. The map above shows Uganda's administrative boundaries as they were at independence in 1962. Amongst all the kingdoms, Buganda is the largest and most central.

The inhabitants of these kingdoms are, with few exceptions, Bantu-speaking peoples. Uganda lies at the northern edge of the vast area of sub-Saharan Africa occupied by Bantu speakers and it is in Uganda, broadly speaking at the River Nile, that the Bantu meet the societies of the north and the Horn of Africa.

... and semi-arid rangelands

North of the Nile, a different ecology prevails. The land stretches away in vast plains; population density is lighter; rainfall is lower and less reliable; surface water becomes more scarce and drought more common. In the north-east region, Karamoja, where the environment is at its most harsh, cattle herding is the most common livelihood. People and animals move with the seasons in search of pasture and water, and there is a limit to the size and duration of settlements. Further west, where the climate allowed the practice of agriculture as well as animal husbandry, patterns of shifting cultivation are common.

▼ A cattle market in Karamoja, northern Uganda, where most people depend on livestock herding for their living

Geoff Sayer

Geoff Sayer

The search for new lands, grass, or water had important impacts on social organisation among these pastoralist groups. Social systems revolved not around kingdoms under the authority of a monarch, but around smaller units such as clans, subject to the authority of a chief or elder, and with leadership based on the achievement of consensus. To this day, eastern Uganda is the most heterogeneous part of the country in terms of its people, languages, and production systems.

Fundamental divisions or common destiny?

The map below portrays the major ethnic groups and languages in Uganda. Bantu languages are confined to the arc around Lake Victoria, while the north and east is a mixture of Sudanic, Nilotic, and Hamitic languages. Bantu speakers comprise about two thirds of the population of Uganda. Their numerical majority helps to explain current patterns of political supremacy; yet a commitment to national unity requires that Uganda's leadership employs specific measures to enable all groups to feel themselves to be equal citizens. If the religious, political, and ethnic divisions which have proved to be so destructive in Uganda are to be reduced and replaced with a stronger sense of nationhood and national identity, the role of economic and social development as a means of minimising differences, rather than accentuating them, will be critical.

For the present, however, this distinction between a northern and eastern bloc and a southern and western bloc remains valid – not least because this divide is most often used by Ugandans themselves to describe their country. In applying this classification, however, there are striking differences of interpretation. For some, the River Nile is a dividing line, a geographical expression of fundamentally different political systems, perspectives, and cultures. For others, the Nile is the common thread, the visible expression of a common destiny that links all Ugandans.

▲ *Longoleluk Kokoi (left) and Maria Keem scrape cow hides. Every part of the hides will be used. The climate and soils of Karamoja do not yield an easy livelihood, and nothing is wasted.*

Language Areas

- Bantu
- Western Nilotic
- Eastern Nilotic
- Sudanic

KAKWA
MADI
LUGBARA
JONAM
ALUR
IK
ACHOLI
KARAMOJONG
LABWOR
TEPETH
LANGI
ITESO
POKOT (SUK)
BANYORO
BASOGA
SEBEI
BAGWERE
BANYOLE
BAGISU
BAAMBA
JAPADHOLA
ITESO
BAKONJO
BATORO
BAGANDA
BAGWE
SAMIA
BANYANKOLE (IRU)
(HIMA)
BAHORORO
BAKIGA
BANYARWANDA

THE RIVER NILE

Mention of the River Nile invariably conjures up pictures of a slow, wide river with palm-fringed banks, and pyramids in the background. In Uganda, think instead of rapids, waterfalls, and white water, interspersed with sections in which the Nile merges into some of Uganda's largest lakes.

The Nile, over 4000 miles in length, is the longest river in the world. It has a number of sources, but its principal one is Lake Victoria – which is itself the world's second-largest freshwater lake. The Nile flows northwards through Uganda and into Sudan. From Khartoum, where the Nile (which in this section is called the White Nile) is joined by the Blue Nile, the river continues its traverse of Sudan before entering Egypt and, eventually, the Mediterranean Sea.

Geoff Sayer

Just below the Nile's outlet from Lake Victoria is the Owen Falls Dam. Built in the 1950s, the dam completely submerged the pre-existing waterfalls of the same name, and in effect converts Lake Victoria into a vast natural reservoir. The dam is, to this day, the only significant hydroelectric power generation facility on the River Nile in Uganda. The river has enormous untapped potential for power generation and a number of schemes – some of them sensitive in environmental terms and at least one of them seriously questioned because of its use of foreign, private capital – are currently under consideration.

▼ *Surrounding regional conflicts mean that there are more than 200,000 refugees from Sudan, Rwanda, and DRC in Uganda today.*

Jenny Matthews

Regional politics – conflict and co-operation

Uganda lies close to the centre of Africa. It is bordered to the east by Kenya – upon which it relies heavily for access to the outside world – and to the south by Rwanda and Tanzania. To the north lies Sudan, a nation which has suffered civil war for much of the last 40 years. This conflict inevitably impacts on Uganda. There are more than 100,000 Sudanese refugees on Ugandan soil. Many of them have been in Uganda for years, and have been settled in permanent sites. The current Ugandan government has expressed support for the right of self-determination of the people of southern Sudan. This position, and the support the government provides to the Sudan People's Liberation Army (the rebel group fighting the government of Sudan) has meant that relations between the governments in Kampala and in Khartoum have often been limited, and characterised by distrust. To the detriment of Uganda's internal security, the Sudan government is actively supporting the Lord's Resistance Army, a rebel group operating in northern Uganda which has perpetrated a war of terror upon the Acholi people for ten years or so.

Running the length of Uganda's western border is the Democratic Republic of Congo, formerly Zaire until the overthrow of the late President Mobutu. Uganda, together with Rwanda, played a leading role in

...DF leave as 'wet chicken', says Nabudere

UPDF pours troops into Kisangani

Uganda pulls away from Tsopo Bridge

▲ *Uganda's involvement in the war in the Democratic Republic of Congo has been heavily criticised from outside Uganda as well as by Ugandans themselves. Momentum grows to end the war, and Uganda - like Rwanda, Zimbabwe, Angola, and Namibia - has begun to withdraw its troops from key locations along the 1500-mile front.*

supporting the insurrection that toppled Mobutu. This support was explained in terms of solving the threat posed by the presence in eastern Zaire (as it was then) of large numbers of Interahamwe (those who were responsible for the genocide in Rwanda in 1994) and remnants of the former Rwandan army. Although the insurrection itself was quickly successful, it equally quickly went wrong. Relations between the new government, led by President Laurent Kabila, and his former allies soured. They turned against him, supporting a second insurrection which has turned into a bitter and complex war of truly international proportions. President Kabila was assassinated in January 2001. One element of the war's complexity is that Rwanda and Uganda – which have enjoyed very close relations in the last ten years – have fought vicious battles with each other in the Congolese town of Kisangani. Uganda's involvement in the war in Congo is extensive and expensive, and it is also largely incomprehensible to most Ugandans. Many believe that it is motivated not by legitimate concerns of national security, but by the personal interests of businessmen and senior army commanders.

The war threatens to sully Uganda's reputation, both regionally and internationally. In addition, the conflict has caused social dislocation, economic disruption, and population displacement in parts of western Uganda of a nature similar to that associated with the insecurity in the north of the country.

Historically, Uganda has been an integral part of East Africa and shares a common colonial heritage with Kenya and Tanzania. Initial attempts to create a regional bloc, the East Africa Community, could not survive the tumultuous years of the 1970s, and it was formally disbanded in 1977. Nevertheless, there are compelling reasons for closer regional collaboration, and the creation of the Commission for East African Co-operation represents a recent and more measured attempt to promote joint initiatives and stimulate the regional economy.

Pre-colonial and colonial Uganda: legacies of the past

Competing for souls and influence

Belief in God – in whatever form – has brought comfort and solace to people of all civilisations. Religion, on the other hand, has played a more problematic role in the history of many countries and peoples, and Uganda is no exception. Christian missionaries were amongst the first Europeans to visit and settle in Uganda, and in some respects they were the front-runners of colonisation. In Uganda's case the coming of Christianity was prompted by an invitation sent in 1875, allegedly on behalf of Muteesa I, the king, or Kabaka, of Buganda. When the letter was published in Britain it prompted a favourable response, and generous donations were made to the Church Missionary Society – a part of the Anglican church – whose missionaries arrived in Buganda in 1877, and have been there ever since. News of the opening up of Buganda to mission activity also attracted the interest of the Roman Catholic church. The contest between Britain and France for influence in Africa meant that the Anglican missionaries were soon followed by a Catholic group, led by French priests. Both denominations began competing for souls and influence.

The initiative of the Christian churches prompted Arab traders to support efforts to introduce Islam. When the Kabaka died in 1884 he was succeeded by his son Mwanga – young, inexperienced, and lacking the leadership qualities of his father. Intrigue and gossip quickly became plotting, and the new Kabaka lost control over his chiefs. In 1888 he was deposed and a series of religious civil wars began. At first the Christian churches and their followers united against the Arab traders and Islam; then they turned on each other. The wars ended in 1892 with a Protestant victory over the Catholics. Kabaka Mwanga was reinstated in 1889, but fled the kingdom in 1892.

▼ A bloody moment in Uganda's history: Hamu Mukasa (1871-1958) narrowly escaped the fate of fellow Christians who died rather than surrender their faith when Kabaka Mwanga II ordered executions of Christian converts in 1885-6. The Catholic victims became known as the Ugandan martyrs.

Geoff Sayer

Because the factions that were battling it out in Buganda were fighting not for the protection of their faith or their right to worship, but for political control of Buganda, these wars had the effect of linking religion and politics in Uganda in a way that has no parallel in other parts of East Africa. From then on, political alignment would be associated with religious persuasion, and as the Uganda protectorate expanded to include territories beyond the kingdom of Buganda this pattern of political alignment was reproduced. By the time independence arrived, all of Uganda's principal political parties were based on religious allegiance, a consequence of the churches' powerful influence over their adherents, and reinforced by the dominant position of religious groups in the provision of education and medical services.

RELIGION IN UGANDA TODAY:
FUSING DIVERSE SPIRITUAL TRADITIONS

The societies of pre-colonial Uganda were deeply spiritual, with a complex array of religious beliefs, practices, and ceremonies. During the course of the last century Christianity, and to a lesser extent Islam, spread quickly, and penetrated all parts of the country. About one third of the population is now Roman Catholic, one third Protestant, and 15-20 per cent Muslim. At the same time, traditional religious beliefs and practices have survived alongside, and even been incorporated into, Ugandans' observance of Christianity and Islam.

In Uganda each tribe has its own ceremonies and rituals for the major life events – birth, marriage, and death – that affect families, households, and clans. These ceremonies are often performed alongside Christian ceremonies. Thus, a traditional marriage will frequently be followed by a church ceremony. Similarly, when someone dies, a church funeral does not replace the observance of mourning rituals and practices derived from an entirely different cultural tradition. It is this capacity to move from one cultural

tradition to another, to recognise the legitimacy of both, and to apply both without any notion of contradiction that gives new meaning to the world 'multicultural'. The Holy Spirit Movement, with an eclectic mix of traditional beliefs and practices and of ideas drawn from its adherents' familiarity with the liturgy of the Catholic church, is an extreme form of this capacity to combine elements of different spiritual traditions into one coherent body of belief.

Geoff Sayer

Geoff Sayer

▲ Britain and Germany competed for power over Uganda in the 'Scramble for Africa', when European countries rushed to claim territory across the continent. Germany ceded its interests to the Imperial British East Africa Company in 1890. In Uganda today, various physical reminders of the colonial past remain.

The statue plaque reads:

MAJOR SIR GERALD PORTAL
BORN 1858 DIED 1894
FROM WHOM THIS TOWN
DERIVES ITS NAME

The seeds of discord

By the middle of the 19th century, when the British and others started to explore East and Central Africa, Buganda was the largest, most sophisticated, and most prosperous of the kingdoms of Central Africa. Its principal rival was Bunyoro to the north-west, and Buganda's early alliance with the British proved to be critical in the subsequent fortunes of these two kingdoms. As a result, Buganda's importance was enhanced, while the status and influence of Bunyoro declined.

Military service had been a legal obligation in Buganda for centuries, and its possession of a standing army equipped with firearms allowed it to extract tribute from some of the neighbouring kingdoms. In addition, a highly developed internal process of wealth generation led to the gradual emergence of artisans manufacturing a wide range of products based on locally available resources.

When the British established the Uganda protectorate in 1894 they built it around Buganda. In the years that followed, other territories were added in a piecemeal process of accretion and military conquest. Bunyoro – the principal threat to Buganda's security and, thus, to British interests – was invaded by a joint British-Baganda force (the people of Buganda are known as the Baganda), and quickly incorporated into the protectorate. The east was also subjugated by a similar combined force.

From the beginning of British rule, then, Buganda had a special place in Uganda. Colonial administration, education, and other forms of 'modern development' began in Buganda and slowly spread outwards to other parts of the protectorate. The evident primacy of Buganda in the eyes of the colonial rulers inevitably affected how the Baganda saw themselves and their kingdom. That primacy was asserted over the rest of Uganda when the British decided to establish a system of administration based on the one they found in Buganda. This system – reflecting as it did a hierarchical society headed by a king – was easily understood and appreciated by the British because it had similarities with their own. But the model was alien to all those parts of Uganda – especially those in the north and east – that had evolved very different social and political structures. For ease of administration the British wanted a single system, and by choosing the one with which the Baganda were most familiar, they were led to employ the Baganda as agents and administrators throughout the country. As a way of putting the administration of the new protectorate

Geoff Sayer

▲ *This palace, at Mengo Hill in Kampala, was the outward expression of the power of the Kabaka of Buganda. After the Kabaka was sent into exile in 1966, the palace became a military barracks. In 1993, President Museveni reinstated the Kingdom of Buganda. The palace was returned to the Kabaka in 1997.*

'on a satisfactory footing' it was very effective. But it left the Baganda feeling as if they were the first amongst equals and generated a corresponding sense of resentment in the rest of Uganda. The seeds of discord had been planted. They would be harvested when Uganda became independent.

'Indirect rule'

The chosen strategy for the administration of Uganda was 'indirect rule' – a euphemism for the creation of a class of collaborators who would be responsible on a day to day basis for the implementation of British rule and who, in return, would enjoy preferential treatment.

With this in mind, the British government negotiated the 1900 Buganda Agreement with the Kabaka and his chiefs. This effectively ended the existence of Buganda as an independent kingdom, in return for which the power of the Kabaka and his parliament was preserved, though made subject to the authority of the protectorate. The architect of the agreement recognised that the 'only people for a long time to come who can deal a serious blow to British rule' in Uganda were the Baganda themselves – hence the need to co-opt them as agents in the creation of a new administrative system, and to reward the chiefs for their compliance. The Buganda Agreement self-consciously and deliberately set out to create a class of notables by parcelling out land to the entire political hierarchy, from the king down to the parish chief, creating a commonality of interest between the British and those who would implement indirect rule.

The next stage was to create a system of local government. When they demarcated the districts that would comprise the basic units of administration, the British tried to ensure that these corresponded with ethnic boundaries as far as possible. There were obvious advantages in adopting a structure that preserved much of what had existed prior to the creation of Uganda. But the one thing such a structure could not and did not do was to create a new sense of common identity, or nationhood.

The energy that went into the creation of an effective system of district government contrasted sharply with the absence or weakness of protectorate-wide institutions of government. For example, the Legislative Council – the precursor of parliament – was set up in 1920, but was composed almost entirely of colonial officials for more than 20 years. The first African members took their seats in December 1945, and even then the Council functioned as a forum in which leaders of local government met to advance their specific district interests, not to formulate national policies. This parochialism was inevitably reflected in the political parties which, by then, were jockeying for position to lead Uganda when it became independent. Initiatives to create genuinely national parties failed to attract the kind of support they needed to be taken seriously, and the political parties that survived the intense competition of the last few years of colonial rule tended to be those that reproduced, rather than rejected, the divisions of colonial rule.

▼ *Although these Acholi children raise the Ugandan flag and sing the national anthem every morning before school, many say that they do not feel part of the Ugandan nation.*

Geoff Sayer

As independence approached, Uganda was best described as a country, but not a nation. The kingdom of Buganda in particular felt angry and betrayed. For so long it had enjoyed a special status, but as the move towards independence gathered momentum, it became clear that the British were determined to hand over power to a central government based on a unitary state. The Buganda parliament was equally determined to do what it could to preserve its identity as a kingdom and, as importantly for the ruling class, to preserve the particular powers of the Buganda parliament (rather than lose them to a national parliament). In 1960, the leaders of Buganda went so far as to declare unilateral independence for Buganda. The policy of divide and rule, practised for nearly 70 years, had been implemented very successfully. But it meant that Uganda's new rulers had a mammoth job to do if they were to succeed in creating a nation state.

Twenty terrible years

Within four years of achieving independence in 1962, Uganda experienced the first of a series of political catastrophes that would make it one of the poorest nations in Africa, and a byword for economic mismanagement, incapable leadership, and the abuse of human rights. Uganda's decline into violence and poverty was marked by the flight of more than half a million of its people, and the murder of a similar number, as successive governments terrorised those communities regarded as being sympathetic to rebels or political opponents. Poverty became so profound that, even 20 years later, the vast majority of Ugandans were measurably poorer than they had been in 1970.

In the run-up to independence, Uganda's politics were so fragmented along tribal and religious lines that the fundamental divide was not between the colonial authorities and a nationalist movement demanding independence; it was a divide between the different elements of the prospective ruling class. The most pronounced of these divisions was between the kingdom of Buganda and the new national government of an independent Uganda. So separate were their interests that they effectively comprised two states within one country. Though the constitution negotiated at independence was described as federal, in reality only Buganda had separate and significant powers. The Buganda parliament (the *Lukiko*) controlled public services and local government, had separate powers of taxation, and its own courts.

▼ These ruins on Mengo Hill in Kampala are testimony to the battle fought in 1966, when Buganda's attempts to become an independent nation were ended.

Geoff Sayer

The Baganda ruling elite had been unable to gain independence for Buganda, but it succeeded in preserving an autonomous economic base, and the political and legal powers to safeguard it.

Political divisions

At independence this fundamental split in the integrity and coherence of the state had been wallpapered over by a marriage of convenience between the Uganda People's Congress (UPC) and the Kabaka Yekka (KY, meaning 'King Only'). The UPC had emerged out of an earlier political grouping, formed by local government leaders outside Buganda to oppose the concessions that Buganda was demanding from the colonial government. The KY represented the Baganda leadership. The purpose of this unlikely alliance was to prevent the success of the Democratic Party (DP) in the elections prior to independence. In power, the spoils of office were divided between the victors. The leader of the UPC, Milton Obote, became Prime Minister, and the Kabaka of Buganda took office as the first President of Uganda. The alliance, however, had nothing to hold it together once the elections were over, and it soon started to fall apart.

The constitution suspended

Things came to a head in 1966. In one corner was Obote with Colonel Idi Amin, the Deputy Army Commander. In the other were the Kabaka of Buganda, the Secretary General of the UPC, and the Army Commander. Amid allegations of coups and counter-coups, Obote and Amin moved more decisively. Obote suspended the constitution, abolished the posts of President and Vice-President, arrested five cabinet colleagues, dismissed the Army Commander, and appointed himself Executive President. A few weeks later he presented an interim constitution at a day's notice that was 'approved' by parliament, though most members present had not seen the document.

The new constitution finished all of Buganda's federally derived powers, ending its financial and political autonomy at one stroke. In a vain attempt to exercise its authority the Buganda Parliament issued an ultimatum, threatening to evict the central government from Buganda's soil within ten days. It was a forlorn attempt to play the 'independence for Buganda' card. The Kabaka had no means of implementing the ultimatum, but it gave Obote his chance. The Kabaka's palace was stormed at the 'Battle of Mengo' and the Kabaka went into exile in Britain. The Kingdom of Buganda was carved up into four districts, and its parliament building was, tellingly, turned into the headquarters of the Ministry of Defence.

Constitutional government, parliamentary democracy, and accountability through the rule of law had effectively ended after just four years, although formally they limped on until 1971. Obote's victory was at least partly due to the fact that he could command the primary loyalty of the army. This was a key lesson of the events of 1966.

In future the power of politicians would increasingly be exercised only with the army's support.

Regional politics in a changing continent

Although the internal dimensions of rivalry and conflict are of paramount importance in explaining Uganda's troubled history, they need to be set in the context of a changing continent. Almost all colonies in Africa became independent between 1956-66. Southern Africa was the exception, and the liberation struggle there was soon to acquire moral, political, and military support from some of the newly independent states. This support was expressed through the formation of the Mulungushi Club, which foreshadowed the creation of the Front Line States as a powerful political bloc, and brought together Kenneth Kaunda of Zambia, Julius Nyerere of Tanzania, Milton Obote of Uganda, and, temporarily, Mobutu of Zaire. It signalled the adoption by Obote of a more radical foreign policy, a change that was also reflected in the development of a closer relationship with President Nimeiry of Sudan.

If the fight against racism dominated politics on the southern borders of the Mulungushi Club members, to the north there was an equally intractable struggle – between Israel and the Arab states, led by Egypt. Because of its dependence on the Nile, Egypt had an obvious interest in creating positive relations with the independent government of Uganda. The conflictual politics between Egypt and Israel meant it was inevitable that Uganda would also be wooed by Israel. Establishing a strong presence in the country as early as 1963, Israel provided assistance to the security forces – training military and police officers, as well as building some of the facilities that would be used by later governments for interrogation and torture.

These changes in foreign policies and alliances were accompanied by changes in economic policy. At a time when the principal cleavage in world politics was between capitalism and communism, the adoption of economic policies characterised by nationalisation and the control of market forces was interpreted as an indication of a political shift to the left. In 1968, when Milton Obote declared his 'Move to the Left' – an extension of state involvement in the economy – western countries too became concerned with events in Uganda. Change was deemed to be necessary, and since Obote had already thwarted attempts by his political rivals using constitutional means, the alternative was to use the army.

▼ The Ugandan national emblem, created for an independent Uganda. The drum on the warrior's shield symbolises the kingdoms and traditions of Uganda, while the sun represents Uganda's equatorial location. Above the shield, ripples indicate Uganda's many lakes, and the water flowing out from below the shield represents the River Nile. The kob and the crested crane are Ugandan native species. Tobacco and cotton plants mingle with the grass.

FOR GOD AND MY COUNTRY

Geoff Sayer

Jenny Matthews

▲ Mass killings and torture became commonplace in Uganda while Amin and his successor Obote were in power. These are skulls of victims of massacres in the Luwero Triangle, where the Obote government was responsible for mass killings of thousands of people between 1981–6. They are a sombre reminder of two decades of violence against Ugandan people.

Amin's coup

The coup happened in January 1971, while Obote was in Singapore attending a Commonwealth Heads of Government meeting. He was informed of the coup by the British Prime Minister, who announced that Idi Amin had taken control of Uganda.

And so it was that the politics of the gun became the dominant politics of Uganda. Concepts of democracy and constitutionalism were abandoned, and the state's responsibility to uphold and protect the civil and political rights of its citizens was turned upside down. Not too many people mourned the demise of their fundamental rights, however – the population of Kampala welcomed Amin as a liberator, while western powers saw in him a loyal ally who could be relied upon in the fight against communism. In Buganda, there was rejoicing at the removal of a man who had expelled and humiliated their king. Cultivating popular support, one of Amin's first acts was to arrange for the return of the late Kabaka's body.

But the dark side to Amin's rule did not take long to emerge. He knew that potential treason was lying in wait in an army that was the creation of Obote. So began the reign of terror for which Amin would become notorious. The first victims were primarily members of the armed forces. They were also primarily people who came from the northern districts of Lango and Acholi. It was a measure of the divisions in Ugandan society that the systematic elimination by Amin of his opponents, real or imaginary, was not greeted with alarm and condemnation. Because the first people to disappear were perceived to be supporters of Obote, this seemed to be sufficient basis for their punishment. Amin's behaviour set a precedent that others would copy in the turbulent years to come.

During the following years, the institutions of government were effectively destroyed. Parliament – weakened even before the coup – was simply abolished. Local government was restructured to enable the government to keep an eye on its political opponents. The civil service became a shadow of its former self. It became increasingly dangerous to offer advice that might be arbitrarily rejected and, as the numbers of civil servants who were 'dismissed in the national interest' increased, morale collapsed. Many Ugandans quietly left the country. But it was the expulsion of the Asians that brought Amin international condemnation.

The expulsion of the Asians

Geoff Sayer

▲ *Some of the families who left Uganda in 1972, expelled by Idi Amin, have now returned. The Ugandan Asians are gradually rebuilding their businesses, such as this shop in Jinja.*

The Asian community in Uganda was the creation of the colonial government. Many of the first immigrants were slave labourers, brought to East Africa from South Asia to build the railway from Kenya; subsequent waves of immigration included skilled artisans. The colonial government would not sell the immigrants land for farming, so they began trading. They were so successful that Asian traders quickly began to dominate the entire commercial sector of Uganda.

Since the 1900 Buganda Agreement there had been a clear division of roles between different population groups in Uganda. Asians were allocated responsibilities for trade, while African farmers were prevented by a variety of regulations from becoming merchants. Because of their non-national status, the Asians were not considered politically threatening. Economically, the great attraction of the traders was that they stimulated an export and import trade that obliterated pre-colonial trading patterns and relationships, and incorporated Uganda into the imperial economy.

After the events of 1966, when Obote appointed himself President, the governing elite had only a limited economic base upon which to operate. Expanding this base was the real objective of the so-called 'Move to the Left' that Obote declared in 1968. By the time of the coup, little progress had been made in implementing those plans. Idi Amin was to choose a more decisive way to address this same problem. Exploiting popular resentment of the Asian community, Amin announced their expulsion. Irrespective of whether they were citizens of Uganda or not, Asians – all 90,000 of them – were ordered to leave. The Asian community was dispossessed of homes, businesses, and property. Shops and warehouses were left full of goods. Amin had not only scored a political goal in favour of 'Africanisation' and as a 'man of action', but he had also given himself the means to control a lucrative network of patronage – dividing the spoils of Asian wealth amongst his supporters.

The economy crumbles…

Spectacular as it was, the precipitate expulsion of a nation's collective capacity of merchants, traders, and industrialists was not a viable policy of economic development. It was the beginning of what was called an economic war, a war that Amin and Uganda's economy – small, and utterly dependent on powerful, global forces – were never going to win. Over the next few years, favoured individuals prospered, but the economy as a whole crumbled. Despite the initial popularity of the policy, many Ugandans now believe that Amin's expulsion of the Asians was the beginning of a prolonged period during which they became poorer, and the nation's public services disintegrated.

... and Uganda goes to war

Against the background of an economy in shambles and an increasingly discontented army, Amin took the risk of securing loyalty to himself by focusing on an external enemy. He invaded Tanzania. The attack was quickly halted and within months the Tanzanians were on the offensive. Amin's troops, heavily armed but poorly trained and unmotivated, retreated and then defected. Amin's army, for so long a source of terror, simply melted away, and when Kampala fell in April 1979, it brought an ignominious end to the rule of the 'Life President and Conqueror of the British Empire', as Amin had styled himself.

Umbrella politics – the Uganda National Liberation Front

Idi Amin had remained in power partly because of the terror his spies inspired in the name of national security, and partly because Uganda's politicians and political activists, many of whom had gone into exile, had been unable to overcome their historical divisions. The Tanzanian counter-offensive, however, marked a turning point, and political groups of one kind or another starting buzzing with activity. After days of squabbling, an umbrella organisation, the Uganda National Liberation Front (UNLF), was born.

▶ *Rusting military relics find a final resting place in the Ugandan countryside. This burnt-out tank was destroyed in the battle between Amin's troops and the Tanzanian army.*

Geoff Sayer

The UNLF was composed of over 20 political and military groups with diverse backgrounds and objectives, and the only thing they had in common was their opposition to Amin. As soon as he had fallen, their differences emerged, and the plotting to replace Yusuf Lule, the man installed as President in April 1979, began soon after he made his first address to the nation. Within weeks, all the groups in the UNLF were at loggerheads, and the 'umbrella' broke into different factions. President Lule lost the confidence of his colleagues and was replaced after just 68 days.

His successor lasted less than a year – not long, perhaps, but with the population suffering extreme harassment and profound fear, and with the economy deteriorating still further, it was a year of unmitigated chaos. Supported by the army, the Chairman of the Military Commission took control of the country.

The return of party-based politics became inevitable. The two big parties – the UPC and the DP – had maintained something of their original structures throughout the previous decade, and were now joined by two new parties. Given that there had been no national elections in Uganda since 1962, and given the disorganisation and fear prevalent throughout Uganda, it was perhaps optimistic to think that democracy, accountability, and the rule of law could be restored simply by holding an election. As polling day grew closer, anxieties began to be expressed that the army would not accept the victory of any party other than the UPC. In the event, the UPC did win, a result that a Commonwealth team of observers concluded fairly reflected the expressed choice of the people. But to this day there are strongly held opinions in Uganda as to the accuracy of that judgement, not least because the Chairman of the Military Commission, who declared Milton Obote the winner, was then himself appointed as Obote's Vice-President and Minister of Defence. To anyone but an avowed UPC supporter, it looked suspicious.

▲ *Women wait to vote at a rural polling station in northern Uganda on 30 September 1980. Milton Obote was elected as President, but the results were widely considered to have been rigged.*

Fiona O'Mahoney

Obote II

From the moment he took office for the second time – Ugandans refer to his first tenure of office as Obote I and to the period between 1980–5 as Obote II – it became clear that the turmoil of the election period would simply continue. Obote's army became a major threat to the civilian population in different parts of the country. Whole communities were seen to be 'the enemy', and the first to suffer were the people of West Nile, in north-west Uganda. Because Amin was from that part of the country, it was judged to be appropriate to punish the whole area, and it was subjected to horrendous levels of violence. Over a quarter of a million Ugandans fled West Nile for Sudan and Zaire.

▲ *Heroes Day, June 9, 1991. President Yoweri Museveni lights a candle in memory of the thousands who were killed during the war in Luwero.*

Jenny Matthews

Guerilla warfare, and the rise of Museveni

At the same time, Yoweri Museveni, a politician who – like Obote – had spent many years in Tanzania in the 1970s, and who had been active in the war against Idi Amin, rejected the election results and started a guerrilla war. His group became known as the National Resistance Movement (NRM), and its army, the National Resistance Army (NRA). Basing itself to the north-west of Kampala in the district of Luwero, the NRA quickly became adept at guerrilla warfare. It hit Obote's army with ambushes and surprise attacks, organised a network of information and support at village level through what were called 'resistance committees', and provoked Obote's army into vicious counter-insurgency operations, further alienating the population from the government, and simultaneously building its own support.

Luwero is in Buganda, and it was the contest between the Baganda and himself that had so dominated Obote's first government. These were his 'old enemies'. But this time the war was much bigger and much dirtier. The Luwero Triangle became synonymous with human rights abuses on a massive scale – killings, torture, rape, extortion, and detentions. Human rights organisations publicised these abuses, and appealed for the upholding of international law, but ultimately it was decisive military action that changed the course of events.

As the guerrilla war extended into other parts of Uganda, so too did the wave of repression. The intimidation reflected the increasing factionalisation of the political and military aspects of public life, which had a strong ethnic dimension. In the south, people of Rwandese origin – Banyarwanda – were particularly targeted. Some had lived in Uganda for many years, having arrived as economic migrants looking for casual work or the opportunity to acquire land. Others were refugees, who had fled Rwanda in the early 1960s. Because Museveni was from a people with some cultural affinity to the Banyarwanda, and because Idi Amin had employed Rwandans extensively in his security forces, all Rwandans became suspected opponents, and tens of thousands of them were expelled from the country. At the time, the plight of these refugees barely registered on the scale of suffering – but the long-term political consequences would be enormous, for it was out of these events that the Rwanda Patriot Front was born, and in less than ten years' time Rwanda itself was at war.

The young, poorly disciplined, and ill-trained troops of Obote's army were increasingly no match for the highly organised, mobile guerrilla fighters. In January 1986, the NRA captured Kampala, and Yoweri Museveni became Uganda's new President. Promising 'fundamental change', Uganda was about to enter a new phase in its social, economic, and political development.

The conflict in the north

When rebels came to our house – Elda Atoo's story

Elda Atoo's house lies on the outskirts of Kitgum town. Made exclusively with locally available materials, it is constructed according to a traditional Acholi design, with a conical thatched roof, and walls of sun-dried bricks. Elda sits in the doorway, in the deep shade of the eaves that provide protection against tropical rainstorms. The compound is quiet in the evening sunshine. It doesn't feel like a house on the edge of a war zone.

Until 1994 Elda, her husband, and his two other wives lived in Padibe, a small town to the north of Kitgum. Then it became too dangerous to stay there any longer. Elda explains:

'We had to sleep in the bush. When the rebels were doing their work, we could not stay in the house. When the sun is almost setting, people from several families move to the bush together. Some stay awake to keep guard. If it rains, like it did last night, you just get wet. And if you have a young baby that cries too much, you are chased away and left to find your own place.

Geoff Sayer

▲ *Elda's daughter Regina is doing well at school, but her domestic responsibilities may mean that she has to give up her education, like many other young women. For now, she is determined to continue.*

'One time rebels came to our house – right into our house. It was 1996 and we were back in Padibe, collecting food. We were about six: me, my husband, and the children. David was outside and saw them coming. He ran away. But they came in without us even seeing. They were suddenly with us in the house, when we looked around. Seven came in. They all had guns. They said, "Sit down!" [Elda mimes a gun, lining up the index fingers of her two hands and pointing across the compound.]

'We were panicking. Shaking. We were so afraid. They were in a hurry and worried about soldiers. "Is the army near?" they asked, "Have you seen soldiers?" They quickly collected things from the house – clothes, blankets, and cooking pots. When they went out, they said, "Now we are leaving you, don't tell anyone that we have passed."

'What we miss most because of the rebels is land,' Elda continues. 'And because we miss land, we miss food.' Elda looks across to the maize growing near the homestead. 'This land is small. Food here would last only one week. We now have famine and disease. The land is there, but we can't go back. If we were at home, we would all be digging now. As a family we could dig five or six gardens in a season. Each garden would have a different crop – millet, sorghum, maize, simsim, groundnuts, beans, and potatoes.'

▲ Elda Atoo sits in the doorway of her house outside Kitgum town. Conflict and displacement create conditions in which disease can spread rapidly. Elda's husband Olal died after developing AIDS in 1997, and Elda also has the illness.

A distant conflict

There are tens of thousands of people like Elda in Kitgum district. Since 1986, Uganda has experienced several internal conflicts, with that in the northern districts of Kitgum and Gulu being the most prolonged and severe. The outcome of this conflict is critically important, and will be an indicator of the NRM's commitment to break the cycle of violence and human rights abuses.

Any visitor to Uganda who has the opportunity to go to the north, as well as to spend time in Kampala and the fertile crescent around Lake Victoria, would be struck by the remarkable contrast between the two. Kampala and the towns of the south and west are thriving. Business is good, and the signs of growth and wealth are evident all around: in the houses being built, the goods available in the shops and markets, and the number of vehicles on the roads. Kampala is one of the safest and most pleasant cities in Africa.

▼ This newly-built hotel in Kitgum town welcomes the influx of NGOs to the district.

Travel north for four to five hours to the town of Gulu, however, and the landscape changes completely. Gulu has also experienced growth in the last ten years, but it is an expansion of cheap investments and hurried construction, signs of flight from an unsafe and increasingly abandoned countryside.

For the residents of southern Uganda, and for tourists and visiting businesspeople, the insecurity and the lack of commercial opportunities lead to a striking lack of contact with northern Uganda. There is remarkably little national concern about the atrocities that are being perpetrated against the people of the north, and an apparent lack of understanding among southern Ugandans about the sheer scale of the humanitarian and economic crisis that has evolved.

▲ *Macleod Baker Ochola II, Anglican Bishop of Kitgum, describes how religious leaders in Kitgum and Gulu districts have joined together to try to end the conflict, forming the Acholi Religious Leaders Peace Initiative.*

Geoff Sayer

The Holy Spirit Movement

Over the last 14 years, the armed resistance to the NRM government has taken various forms. In its early stages there is no doubt that it received widespread and voluntary support. In 1987, Alice Lakwena – a young woman with no previous military experience – became the leader of an armed opposition group called the Holy Spirit Movement (HSM). The HSM was a complex movement combining political and military opposition to the Museveni government with a mission to cleanse the Acholi themselves of the sins they had committed in earlier wars. The Catholic Bishop of Gulu and Kitgum expressed this in his 1987 Easter homily, when he spoke of the atrocities in the Luwero Triangle:

'Many joined the army with the hope of getting rich overnight, and were used by unscrupulous political leaders who sent them to carry out "operations" in areas of political unrest. These operations involved atrocious acts of violence against innocent civilians, including children and women, who were subjected to unspeakable mistreatment. A lot of looting was done.... When the loot was brought home, parents and relatives welcomed it in their homes, knowing that it was looted. Instead of correcting their children and condemning their actions, many parents had only praise for them. We can now see that these present sufferings are the result of our own sin.'

These communal senses of guilt and of confession among the Acholi contributed to the emergence of the Holy Spirit Movement. It had potent appeal, combining elements of Christianity with traditional beliefs. Alice was a charismatic leader, and was perceived to have the power 'to cure illness in society' and to purify her followers.

Within a year, the Holy Spirit Movement was shattered, destroyed by the National Resistance Army (NRA), determined to overcome the legacy of a series of earlier embarrassing defeats. In an astute political move, the NRM offered an amnesty to another of the rebel groups; this persuaded the vast majority of them, tired and disillusioned, to come out of the bush and to return from camps in Sudan where they were hiding.

The cattle warriors

At the same time as the Holy Spirit Movement was challenging the NRA, the ordinary farmers of Kitgum and Gulu were being subjected to attacks, not by the army, but by warriors from Karamoja.

For generations, cattle have been the store of wealth for the Acholi people. Their cattle are used to fulfil social obligations, such as the provision of dowry when one of their children marry. Cattle may also be used as a bank, to be drawn upon in times of drought or illness, or to meet the costs of education. By 1986 their collective stock of some 250,000 cattle represented their principal asset.

The Karimojong – the people of Karamoja – have an uneasy relationship with the Acholi. Dependent on access to the pastures and

▲ *For many northern Ugandans, cattle are a store of wealth: the equivalent of savings, insurance, or a pension.*

water of Acholi in the dry season, the Karimojong nevertheless have a long history of cattle raiding in Kitgum's eastern counties. In 1987 there occurred a series of Karimojong raids that had no precedent. The effects were truly devastating for the local economy. Huge numbers of well-armed Karimojong swept though the whole of Kitgum, and most of neighbouring Gulu too. Almost the entire stock of Acholi wealth – all 250,000 cattle – was taken.

At a stroke, the productive base of the Acholi rural economy was removed wholesale – savings, oxen, and milk herds. No restitution has ever been paid to the Acholi. This, and the fact that the police and the military authorities made no attempt to stop the Karimojong, led to a widespread suspicion among the Acholi that raiding on such a scale could not have occurred without the approval of the authorities. Indeed, it is now becoming accepted that the army was involved in the raiding. The Ugandan government is ultimately responsible for the security of its citizens and their property, and its failure to fulfil its responsibilities is the source of a deep and continuing bitterness among the Acholi. The Bishop of Kitgum makes an unfavourable comparison: 'Amin's reign of terror affected the military, the civil servants, but it did not really affect ordinary people. That's the difference with this government. They have destroyed our wealth – our cattle, granaries, and houses. The cattle rustling of the Karimojong was the first step in a process that has left the Acholi people deep in the pit of poverty.'

The Lord's Resistance Army

With the Holy Spirit Movement defeated, there arose a brief opportunity to bring the rebellion to an end. Instead, however, a small, hard-core group of rebels from different movements eventually came together under the leadership of Joseph Kony, calling themselves the Lord's Resistance Army (LRA). Like Alice Lakwena, Kony claimed to be possessed by religious powers that were using him as their medium. There the comparison with Lakwena ends, however. From the beginning, the LRA has appeared to be driven by quite different motives. It seems to have no political agenda, and does not offer any alternative analysis on key issues of social, economic, or political development.

Instead of winning the 'hearts and minds' of the Acholi people, the LRA's behaviour is violent, unpredictable, and arbitrary. The LRA has

Geoff Sayer

▲ At Pandwong School in Kitgum, crowded classes like this have become normal since the rebel attacks and abductions began. Most of the schools in the area have been closed, and children are sent to towns, where they can attend school and face less risk of abduction.

consistently committed serious human rights abuses against civilians. In the early 1990s it would frequently maim its victims by cutting off their ears, lips, or legs with machetes. Whereas the Holy Spirit Movement engaged in battle with the NRA, the LRA appears to minimise its contact with the army. During more than ten years of war, it has never mounted an attack on the army barracks in Kitgum, for example. Instead, it preys upon civilians, on villages, on the unarmed; it attacks schools, health centres, or passing vehicles. In a report on the human rights violations of the LRA, Amnesty International observed that in Gulu district in July and August 1996, 11 teachers and over 100 children were killed, 250 primary school children abducted, and 59 primary schools burnt down. This led to the closure of 136 out of the district's 180 primary schools. In the words of investigating parliamentarians, 'There is hardly any meaningful education going on in the north.'

The LRA claims to be resisting on behalf of the Acholi, but its actions appear to be confined to terrorising the population. In the absence of popular support, the LRA survives by the use of a cruel strategy – the capture and servitude of children and young people. In addition, the LRA receives material and military support from the government of Sudan, and its principal purpose seems to be to act as a militia to combat the Sudanese People's Liberation Army (SPLA) on behalf of the Sudan Army. Amnesty International reports the case of one abductee who took part in three joint operations with the Sudan Army against the SPLA. Another abductee commented that, 'Many of the soldiers fighting the SPLA were Ugandans.'

Geoff Sayer

Geoff Sayer

▲ *The Kicwa Centre in Kitgum acts as a refuge and rehabilitation centre for child abductees who have escaped. The children arrive at the centre after extremely traumatic experiences. Drawings and paintings like these, as well as discussion, form part of their rehabilitation.*

Abduction

Fear of abductions is all-pervasive in the north. Children are terrified of being captured, and parents live in fear of seeing their children killed or taken away by rebels. After so many years of war, the adoption by the LRA of a strategy of abduction, and the reluctance of the government to seek a realistic, negotiated peace, have created a widespread feeling of hopelessness and despair among the Acholi. People see no end to their suffering. They feel there is little they can do to stop the war. To reduce or limit the effects of the war on their families, people move out of the district if they can, or send their children to school outside the district. If that is not possible, children are sent to stay with relatives and friends in Kitgum and Gulu towns. As a last resort, people sleep in the bush, cultivate a few fields close to their houses, and hide whenever there is a hint of danger.

According to the Justice and Peace Committee in Kitgum, the number of children and adults who have been abducted is likely to exceed 20,000. According to Amnesty International, over 2000 children were abducted from four parishes in 1995 alone.

And in an exceptional piece of original, community-based research, a women's organisation in Kitgum reconstructed the history of all abductions to have occurred in just one trading centre, Omiya Anyima. From just one settlement a total of 272 people (63 of them female) have been abducted since 1995.

Of those abducted, just 64 returned home alive. Another 39 are known to have been killed – and that leaves the vast majority, 169 people, simply missing.

The stories of abducted children can be heard, day after day, in town and village, from all kinds of people – pupils, teachers, parents in feeding centres, and displaced families. Collectively, they provide consistent and overwhelming evidence of one of the most grotesque forms of insurgency and political opposition.

Here is the testimony of three children who experienced abduction. Their real names have to be omitted in order to protect them: we shall call them Ben, Jack, and Sarah.

Ben's story

'I stay in Kitgum with my aunt. My parents live 24 kilometres away in Latanya. I haven't been there for eight years, because there are a lot of rebels. They have taken a lot of children. They took me.

'I was arrested in 1997, when I was ten. I was with them for five months. We patrolled in Kitgum district and in Sudan. We were taken from school when we were playing football. We were eight – boys and girls. I am the only one who has come back; the rest are in Sudan, or have been killed.

'I planned how to escape. When they slept, I began to wake up. We were in the bush. We sleep close together, but I wasn't afraid. I didn't run – I walked, quietly. There was no moon, or I wouldn't have tried to escape.

'It had not been possible to get away earlier. They tie you up for a month. You are tied even when you go to the toilet. We all talked of escaping, but we were afraid. If they catch you, they will just kill you – always. Two tried to escape from my group, and were killed. And most parents are killed [at the time of the abduction]. If you escape, you have no family to go to.

'I escaped because I had to carry heavy loads. I missed my parents, and I missed having clothes and food. We were hungry. Sometimes we didn't eat. We had to find food by going to people's homes and taking it. It was difficult living in the bush. When it rains you just sleep the same way, out in the bush, and get wet.'

Jack's story

▲ Jack completes a maths exercise in his class at Pandwong School, Kitgum. Like many of the pupils at the school, Jack managed to escape after being abducted by the rebels.

'I was taken in 1995, when I was ten,' Jack explains, 'We lived 18 kilometres from Kitgum, in Acholibur. It was at night, when we were asleep. Three of us were taken. After we'd been caught we were tied up like slaves. I was with the rebels one year and eight months before I escaped.

'We were taken to Sudan for training, after two or three months I was given a gun. Then we were sent into Kitgum district and that's where I learned to use it. They left us without food, and then we were sent into Kitgum district where we had to take food from the villagers. Our group was 20 strong. We had a radio, and communicated with other units.

'I was afraid to try to escape, in case they caught me and killed me. I saw many children killed. They are killed with a machete to the head. It happened all the time. They make children kill other children. I had to kill other children, or they would have killed me.

'I have forgotten it all now. I want to forget. For them the gun is a very good thing. The gun makes people fear you. When I was there I thought the gun was good. Now I think it brings more problems than solutions.

'The rebels' purpose is to capture people – children – to increase the number of soldiers. They want to destroy people's property. Sometimes we were told to kill people, sometimes we were forbidden to kill people. It changed from mission to mission. We were told that if we followed instructions, we would be protected, no harm could come to us.'

Sarah's story

Sarah writes an essay in her class at Pandwong School, Kitgum. Like other escaped abductees, she lives in fear. If the rebels recapture her, they will kill her.

Geoff Sayer

'I was taken in 1994, when I was 13. I was at home in Wol. Seven of us were taken, four boys and three girls. I was with the rebels for two years.

'They came at night. They banged at the door. We were sleeping, three of us. They said, "Come out!" We walked out. We were scared. We knew it must be the rebels. I said, "I'm not going anywhere, I am staying." They said they would kill me if I didn't go with them. The man didn't shout, he just spoke normally. I knew it was true. My father came out, but he could only watch. He cried for me. He just had to stand as we left.

'We walked all night, without resting. We kept walking the next day, carrying heavy loads. One boy tried to escape, but they caught him easily. They brought him back. He was crying. They shot him. They made us watch. They shot him in the head.

'After about a week I had to become the wife of a soldier. That's what happens to the girls. We went to Sudan. We were trained, and eventually I was given a gun and uniform. We were divided into 20 groups of about 15. We were all girls. We were given missions in Kitgum district. We always had to find our own food. Kony comes to address troops returning to Uganda. The young ones are supposed to lower their eyes, not to look at him. You have to obey the Spirit's command. For example the Spirit may say, "You must not kill any chicken for the next three weeks. Then after three weeks, when you kill a chicken, then you can start killing people."

'I escaped on one of our missions. Our group was told to go to a trading centre to take food, money, and children. I had my friends. They said, "Sarah, today, let's escape." I said, "No. I don't know this place." I persuaded my friends to move towards another centre that I knew. In the end only three of us escaped. The others said they wouldn't go back because their parents weren't there – they were dead. That's why the rebels kill parents.'

MATO OPUT: RECONCILIATION AMONG THE ACHOLI

As a way of helping people to seek forgiveness and reconciliation when a wrong has been done, the Acholi have developed the ritual of Mato Oput – based on drinking from a common vessel.

Mato Oput is a ritual for reconciliation. It is based on the principle that forgiveness is more important than revenge. In order for reconciliation to take place, the offender must accept responsibility for their deeds, and the victim's family must accept, as a gesture of goodwill, an offer of compensation. The Mato Oput ceremony is designed to remove both the anger of the aggrieved and the guilt of the offender.

The ceremony of Mato Oput begins when the two affected clans meet on opposite sides of a dry riverbed. Under leadership of the elders of both clans, a small group meets in the riverbed and a sheep or goat is killed. It is cut in half. One clan takes one half of the animal to be cooked and the other clan takes the other half. Traditional beer is then prepared, and the pounded leaves of the oput plant are put into the beer. Oput is a very bitter plant and the bitterness of the plant is intended to reflect the bitterness caused by the crime. Opposing clan members come to drink from a gourd containing the beer. They crawl on their knees towards the gourd, face each other, touch heads, and, with their hands tied behind their backs, drink from the gourd. Every member of the clan will come to drink. When this is completed there is joint feasting, and from that day on there must be no future reference to the crime that was committed.

Internal displacement

Sometime after Elda Atoo and her family decided to leave Padibe, the area suffered a wave of violence, terrible even by the standards of this war. In a series of massacres in early January 1997, parts of Kitgum district were systematically attacked by the LRA. The massacres went on for four nights, and over 400 men, women, and children were hacked to death. Thousands of homes were looted and burned. As word of what was happening spread, the civilian population fled in panic. They fled to small trading centres, such as Padibe, where there was a mission and a small detachment of soldiers. Three years later, the displaced people's camp is still there.

According to Amnesty International's 1999 Annual Report, over 400,000 people are internally displaced in Gulu and Kitgum. Many have expressed a wish to return to their villages, but have been prevented from doing so by the authorities.

A divided existence

Most of the people in the camp live a divided existence. Those who live relatively close by – within six miles or so – will try to return to their homes during the day to check that everything is okay. They will work in their fields, both as a means of maintaining their independence and dignity, and in order to supplement the limited rations distributed by the World Food Programme. Others, who came to the camp from more distant villages, have to look for land to use or rent in the vicinity of the trading centre, or do casual work such as collecting water or making bricks. As the camp secretary, George Opokotoo says, 'People want to go back home because at this time of year [June] they should be cultivating. It is hard to get land in the trading centre and even if you do get some and plant, there's a danger that the owner will take the land back just as you are about to harvest.'

Geoff Sayer

▲ *Teodora Amono cleans maize at Padibe displaced camp in Kitgum district. The camp is now home to 30,000 people.*

Nobody would choose to live in a displaced persons' camp. They contain no amenities whatsoever and do not even provide a guarantee of protection. In March 2000, Padibe camp was itself attacked by the rebels. Seven hundred houses were burned down, 38 people were injured, and 13 people killed.

The displaced camps in the north are also known as protected villages. In certain circumstances, and Padibe was one, they may be created in response to flight from the rebels. But in other cases, villagers have been encouraged by the army to leave their homes and to move into these protected villages. In neither case is the displacement voluntary. Staying in a protected village in reality provides little protection and for many people spells economic devastation, primarily because they do not have access to land. On the other hand, if they go back home, villagers fear attack by rebels, or of being seen as sympathetic to the rebels by the army. Caught in the middle of military strategies from both sides, the villagers do not know which way to turn.

▼ *Women in Kitgum making a little money by selling rice and banana cakes. Like others, they face the challenge of maintaining their livelihoods despite displacement and continuing insecurity.*

Geoff Sayer

Fighting HIV and AIDS in Uganda

Jenny Matthews

▲ William seeking help from Kitovu Hospital's mobile health programme in 1991. Dying of AIDS, he was desperate to find someone who would look after his six year old daughter Maria.

Approximately 34 million men, women, and children today suffer from an illness that was unknown just 20 years ago. That illness is HIV/AIDS. Almost 70 per cent of the global total of HIV-positive people live in sub-Saharan Africa.

Whilst in Europe and North America, AIDS is often perceived to be a disease of minorities, such as gay men or injecting drug users, in Africa it is the opposite. AIDS has affected millions of households, and the principal means of transmission is heterosexual intercourse. In the last 20 years, millions of people have died, and AIDS is now the most common cause of death amongst adults in Africa. Because AIDS tends to be most prevalent amongst the working population – those between 15 and 50 years of age – it causes poverty and destitution for their families and dependents.

Uganda was one of the first countries in Africa to be hit by AIDS. Originally called 'slim' because of the wasting effect it has on the body, it was the subject of fear and superstition when it first appeared in the early 1980s. In this climate, the government of Uganda took an unusual and brave step. At a time when HIV and AIDS were still poorly understood, and considered by some to be a 'deviants' plague', the Minister of Health travelled to the World Health Assembly in 1986 and spoke publicly about the extent and nature of AIDS in Uganda.

So Strong, So Smooth it really...

feels good PROTECTOR

Geoff Sayer

▲ *Increasing condom use is an important part of Uganda's fight against HIV and AIDS.*

This marked an important turning point. In the same year, Uganda established a National AIDS Control Programme that brought together government, donors, religious organisations, and charities. The government's response was based on a recognition that AIDS affects all strata of the population, and poses a major threat to the development of the country and the welfare of its people. The result has been a policy characterised by openness, an integrated approach to care and prevention – as opposed to treating AIDS only as a medical problem – and a readiness to include a wide range of organisations in policy definition and implementation. A national HIV sero-survey was commissioned in 1988, followed by the establishment of an effective system for monitoring the spread of the disease. The first AIDS referral clinic was created at Mulago Hospital in Kampala in 1987, and the first voluntary counselling and testing facility was opened in 1990.

The Kitovu 'mobile'

Pioneering community-based projects recognised at a very early stage the critical importance of providing ongoing support to relatives and dependants of those suffering HIV/AIDS, many of whom might be carers, or bereaved. The Kitovu outreach project, known as 'the mobile', comprises three components – home care and treatment for those infected; care and support for orphans; and education. The current director of the Kitovu project, Robina Ssentongo, joined the project in 1989 and remembers her early experiences vividly.

'I started by working with AIDS patients. I remember those first few visits, when the woman I was working with took me to a house.... A man came out and he was very tall, but he was so thin, so very, very thin. If you were not strong, you would run away from the house. Whenever I think of HIV/AIDS that man comes back to my mind .... There have been many others, but he was the first I saw.'

Geoff Sayer

▲ *Robina Ssentongo confronts the impacts of AIDS every day in her work.*

'Another memory I have is my first encounter with orphans, because I am the one who started the orphans programme. I remember how miserable they were. I remember I used to dance with them, and jump, to make them cheerful, to try to make them happy. They used to call me mother, and even now some still call me mummy. Those memories connect in my mind to my own children and I think if I were to leave my children at that age, would they have a chance of someone coming in and being concerned about them, to pay their school fees, make sure they're happy and have food at home?'

The scale of the problem that confronts people like Robina every day is reflected in appalling statistics. The number of people with HIV/AIDS in Uganda is estimated to be 1.9 million, including about ten per cent of the adult population. AIDS is the leading cause of death among 15–19 year olds. In 1999 alone, over 100,000 people in Uganda are estimated to have died of AIDS-related illnesses.

TASO: 'LIVING POSITIVELY AND DYING WITH DIGNITY'

The Aids Support Organisation (TASO) has its origins in a small group of people who began to meet informally in 1986. It was a mixed group, made up of a lorry driver, two soldiers, an accountant, a nurse, and a teacher amongst others. Although they were all practising Christians, they decided from the beginning to make TASO a non-religious organisation. Its 17 founding members included 12 who had HIV or AIDS. All of them have since died.

TASO's founding members had no training in counselling or experience of managing an AIDS support group. There were no precedents for such groups in Uganda from which they could learn. They had no funds and no office. What they did have in abundance was vision, initiative, and a commitment to practical action. Under their slogan, 'Living positively and dying with dignity', TASO began to try to change attitudes, and to undermine the climate of silence and fear which impeded discussion and generated prejudice.

Noerine Kaleeba was the first director of TASO. Her husband, Chris, was taken ill while studying at Hull University in the United Kingdom. 'The British Council brought me to be with Chris while he was in hospital. He was the first AIDS patient at Castle

Hill Hospital and the staff were marvellous, so kind and compassionate. I met the 'buddy group' [volunteers who provide support and counselling to people with HIV or AIDS] and for three weeks Chris, our buddy, and I talked of nothing else. The idea of TASO originated from the example of the doctors and nurses who looked after Chris in Britain, the kindness and care they showed him, and from what we had seen of the Terrence Higgins Trust and the buddy system of counselling.'

TASO provides a counselling service to its clients and runs day centres where clients and their families can meet, providing support to relatives and dependants as well as those with HIV and AIDS. TASO actively recruits educators and counsellors who are HIV-positive, so that the advice and support it offers is based on people's real experiences.

Today, AIDS service organisations of all kinds cover activities from awareness promotion to the provision of legal advice. The techniques they use – such as drama, and the use of celebrities, advertising, and radio – are designed to be popular, eye-catching, capable of reaching large audiences, and effective in understanding and changing behaviour.

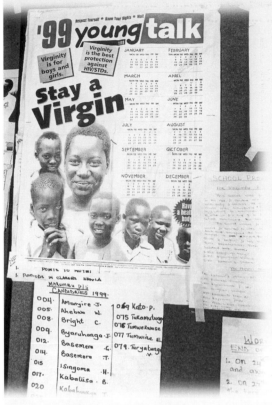

Geoff Sayer

The patterns of transmission of HIV and AIDS are not the same amongst men and women. For biological reasons, women of all ages are more likely than men to become infected with HIV during unprotected intercourse, and the risk of this happening is greater in younger women. This biological vulnerability can combine with social, cultural, and economic factors to increase the likelihood of women and girls becoming HIV-positive. In Uganda, as in many countries, gender discrimination means that, overall, women have a lower social status than men. For many women, this reduces their power to make decisions and to act independently, as a result of poverty and economic dependence on men. Girls may become coerced into sex, or be obliged to trade sex for economic survival. It is common for girls to become sexually active earlier than boys, and usually with a partner older than they are. The rise of HIV and AIDS causes this pattern to become even more pronounced. Older men are breaking long-established social customs and are choosing younger and younger girls to be their sexual partners, in order to avoid catching HIV. In so doing they are in fact infecting them. In Masaka, HIV prevalence among 13–19 year old girls is at least ten times higher than in males of the same age.

Despite the commitment of the government and donors, and the innovative approach, success in combating HIV has not been achieved easily. During the late 1980s, the prevalence rate increased threefold in just five years. Many people were afraid of this new and devastating disease, and their fear fed widespread prejudice. Those who had HIV were seen to be a threat to their families and to the wider community. Discrimination and rejection were widespread. Many people expressed the view that to care for AIDS sufferers was a waste of resources because 'they were going to die anyway'.

The readiness of the government to acknowledge the scale and nature of the problem, and in particular its readiness to open up a debate about sexual behaviour, has been critically important. It allowed the emergence of a network of AIDS support organisations whose influence has been exceptional. Many of these organisations are rooted in the churches' history of care and service. The earliest and best-known examples were initiated by Catholic nuns at hospitals in Kampala and Kitovu. But perhaps the most significant of all has been the emergence of TASO, which has grown to become a nationwide organisation with an international reputation.

Geoff Sayer

▲ *Molly Nantongo in 1994, shortly after her parents' deaths, peeling sweet potatoes for her family's evening meal*

▼ *'Things are changing': Molly and her husband Jackson look towards an AIDS-free future.*

Geoff Sayer

Molly Nantongo's story – how AIDS impacts on families

The family of Molly Nantongo is one of those assisted by the Kitovu project. Molly's mother died in 1992. 'My mother had swellings on her body and developed a fever. My father took her to clinics where she got injections and tablets. He paid a lot of money, but I don't know how much. When she became too sick to go, father brought the medicine home and I cleaned the wounds. Some of her friends also helped.'

A year later Molly's father died too. Molly was just 17 and was now the head of the family, responsible for five younger sisters and brothers, and for a half-sister whose mother had also died.

At first, Molly was determined to continue with schooling for herself and her siblings. The Kitovu project paid her school fees but for all their other needs they had to depend on themselves. By getting up at five in the morning and working on their land before going to school, they grew enough food to eat and to enable them to buy salt, kerosene, matches, and soap. But the burden of caring for her younger brothers and sisters, of being responsible for the house, and of trying to study at the same time – Molly had once remarked how she wanted to be a nurse at Kitovu if she got good marks – was too much for her. The death of both parents within a year had shaken the very foundations of family life. Reluctantly, Molly left school. 'It was too much. I couldn't continue. At home I had no problem – I could always cook and dig. But at school I worried all the time about home, and decided to concentrate on looking after the children.'

Molly married in 1996, a new beginning after the trauma of her teenage years. She now has two children of her own. Two of her sisters have also married. It is common for children deprived of one family to move quickly to create another for themselves. The effects of their parents' death can be seen on other members of the family too. Molly's youngest brother, who was just eight years old when his father died, became unruly and disruptive in school. He dropped out before completing primary school, has become withdrawn, and lives on his own in his family's old house.

The National Community of Women living with HIV/AIDS in Uganda (NACWOLA), is the only national NGO run for, and by, HIV-positive women in Uganda. Initially, NACWOLA was intended to enable HIV-positive women to provide one another with emotional support and practical assistance. However, many NACWOLA members also feel it is their duty to speak publicly about living with HIV. It takes enormous courage to talk about one's HIV-positive status at a church, in a workplace, or in a community meeting. As Beatrice Were, the co-ordinator of NACWOLA, explains, 'People often think, when they see us speaking in public, that we must be very brave. They don't realise that we feel a lot of pain when we do that because we are risking our families, our friends, and our jobs. When you speak in public about living with HIV, your life changes forever. People no longer see you for what you are. They start referring to you as "that woman with AIDS".... So you need a lot of emotional support, you need friends who appreciate you for who you really are.

'But even those of us who speak in public find it difficult to discuss our HIV status with our children.

The fact that, in Africa, we traditionally do not talk openly with our children about sensitive issues like sex and death makes this hard. Also, AIDS prevention messages aimed at the general public often portray people with HIV/AIDS as being promiscuous and immoral. This makes it even more difficult for us to [talk] because they have been made to believe that AIDS affects only morally bad people.

'The children of parents with HIV are often last to be told that there is HIV in the family. They are left to guess, or to learn from rumours, why mummy or daddy is often sick, or behaving strangely. We think that children have a right to know and should not be left in the dark to worry by themselves.'

NACWOLA is pursing a number of imaginative ways of helping HIV-positive mothers to prepare their children for a time when they will have to cope without parental guidance and support. Initiatives include introducing children to future carers, and providing them with detailed information about themselves, their backgrounds, and their families.

Geoff Sayer

Changing behaviour and HIV infection rates in Uganda

Uganda is widely considered to be one of the few success stories in Africa in developing an effective response to HIV and AIDS. The early investment in creating a system to monitor HIV infection means that Uganda has reliable information on the scale of the epidemic, on trends in HIV prevalence, and on behavioural change.

The estimated prevalence of HIV infection in Uganda peaked at about 30 per cent in the early 1990s. By 1999 it had fallen to 12 per cent. Infection rates amongst the young have been significantly reduced – from 28 per cent of females under 20 years of age in 1991 to just six per cent in 1998. Behind these statistics are profound and rapid changes in attitudes and behaviour.

These changes have been witnessed by people like Maurice Ssali who has worked with the Kitovu project for over 11 years. It was Maurice who helped Molly when she nursed her dying parents, and later as she brought up her younger brothers and sisters. For Maurice, the biggest change is that young people are increasingly using condoms. In a 1995 survey of Ugandan adolescents, 36 per cent of boys and 25 per cent of girls reported using condoms, as compared to 15 per cent and seven per cent respectively in 1989.

In addition, young people are waiting till later to begin having sex. The proportion of girls and boys aged 15–19 who have not had sex rose from 20 per cent in 1990 to 50 per cent in 1995.

▲ *Maurice has seen improvements since the early 1990s, when his district had the highest HIV infection rate in the world. These changes are reflected in nationwide studies, which show a significant decline in infection rates.*

Maurice observes how beliefs and attitudes around HIV and AIDS are also changing. 'At first families thought it was witchcraft – you were cursed, then neglected. When you died they threw away your clothes. They would not sit on the chair you used to sit on. That is changing. Belief in witchcraft is still there but family members don't neglect them.'

Uganda's first AIDS cases were identified in Rakai district, where Molly lives. By the late 1980s the area had one of the highest HIV infection rates in the world. At last, Molly feels the situation is improving. 'We bury fewer people these days. Behaviour has changed. Many teenagers were getting pregnant, but now that happens to only a few. People talk about AIDS openly – at funerals, in church, and children are taught about it at school. The friends I grew up with in primary school are alive and well. Some still study, some are at home, some are married. But none has died of AIDS.'

Karamoja:
the rangelands of the north

Karamoja occupies the north-eastern corner of Uganda, bordered to the north by Sudan and to the east by Kenya. Karamoja is semi-arid and more prone to drought than any other part of Uganda. It is dominated by plains of savannah grasslands, vast and sparsely wooded, which join with the sky in a haze of heat and dust.

The name Karamoja originates from a group of people collectively called the Karimojong who live in Moroto district. Now the name is widely used to refer to all of the peoples of the north-east who are primarily livestock keepers. Most Karimojong are cattle herders, although the cultivation of crops (especially sorghum) is also important within the household economy. Men live for extended periods in cattle camps that move according to the availability of pasture and water, and to avoid cattle raiding by neighbours. Women, and their families, tend to remain in the permanent settlement or village. These settlements may comprise as many as 20 or more households that have chosen to live together for reasons of security and the provision of mutual support.

▶ Division of labour among the Karimojong: while young men tend the cattle in mobile herds, women grow crops like sorghum and millet.

Geoff Sayer

What makes Karamoja different?

The Karimojong are the only group of peoples in Uganda who live as semi-nomadic herders. Mobility is an essential part of their way of life. This mobility brings with it the potential for conflict, with other groups of Karimojong or with neighbouring peoples, over access to land, and competition for natural resources such as water and grazing.

Karamoja has experienced prolonged social and political isolation as well as economic marginalisation. As long ago as 1911, Karamoja was declared a closed zone, and administered under restrictions reminiscent of a state of emergency. Even in the 1950s, outsiders needed a permit to enter Karamoja from other parts of Uganda. Things did not improve with independence. Mutual mistrust, prejudice, and a lack of understanding have continued to define relations between the Karimojong and outsiders in general, and the government in particular.

The rangelands of East Africa are home to some of the most spectacular wildlife on earth. This led the colonial government of Uganda to demarcate large slices of Karamoja and classify them as game park, game reserve, or controlled hunting areas. Grazing and settlement were prohibited, and offenders could be imprisoned or have their animals confiscated. The Karimojong were unique amongst Ugandans in having so much of their land placed under such extensive restrictions and controls. They resented this interference deeply, primarily because it prevented them from using land and water resources according to seasonal demands and traditional management arrangements. To the Karimojong it appears that essential resources such as dry season pastures and water holes are reserved for the preferential use of wild animals, at the expense of the survival of their livestock.

The attitudes and values of the Karimojong to 'western' education also distinguish them from the majority of Ugandans. Regarded as the basis for participation in national life, education – in the form of schooling – has spread quickly in Uganda and has become highly valued. In Karamoja, however, it has been widely perceived to be a threat to traditional values and the cohesion of Karimojong culture. This rejection of schooling illustrates

▼ When times are hard, farmers are forced to sell their cattle just when prices are at their lowest.

Geoff Sayer

Geoff Sayer

▲ *Aerobic exercise for Tino at the hand-pump. Water is a scarce commodity in the dryest part of Uganda.*

the Karimojong's fierce determination to defend their way of life with little regard for their common nationality with the other peoples of Uganda.

Successive central governments – from colonial times until today – have been unable to assert their control over the Karimojong. This is reflected in the fact that they are permitted to carry weapons in a way that would not be tolerated anywhere else in Uganda. Their possession of weapons is strongly resented by other Ugandans. In colonial times, the Karimojong carried spears, but since the late 1970s they have acquired a huge armoury of automatic weapons. For this reason they are widely feared by those communities who suffer the oppression of armed attacks against which they do not have the means to defend themselves. Their neighbours – the Acholi, Langi, and Itesot – do understand the need of the Karimojong for migration in years of drought, and invariably accommodate their arrival. Nonetheless, there are many stories of families helping Karimojong migrants during the dry season only for warriors of the same clan to return later to loot, and even kill, their erstwhile hosts.

The Karimojong are a social and political minority, have a lifestyle that few outsiders sympathise with, and are victims of stereotypes and prejudice. Many people recognise this. Nonetheless, their unprovoked and violent attacks on their neighbours tend to destroy feelings of understanding and goodwill and lead to pressure on the government to 'do something about the Karimojong'.

Violence in Karamoja

The Karimojong incursions into neighbouring districts attract most public attention. However, far more serious in terms of the frequency and violence of attacks are conflicts between different sections of the Karimojong themselves. These conflicts have a long history, reflected in Karimojong mythology and legend. Nonetheless, the nature of these conflicts has been changing considerably over the past two generations.

Geoff Sayer

▲ *Lorochom, an elder, reflects on the destructive developments in Karimojong raiding culture.*

One Karimojong warrior, aged 54, explains, 'During our times, raiding was once in a while. This was when disease attacked our 'kraal' and we lost all the cattle. I started thinking day and night when all our livestock were dead. I had planned to marry that year. So when other youth said they were going for a revenge raid in Turkana for the livestock which were lost three years before, I supported them quickly, so that I would try my luck at building up our livestock again.

'For that raid we were a group of 42 men, all with spears, shields, and sticks for driving animals. We were successful. We raided 151 head of cattle, which were distributed amongst us all. I received ten; others received various numbers, with at least one animal for everyone. When we came back, the villagers welcomed us. Our mothers sprinkled our bodies with water using coach grass. The elders were given an ox to roast. None of us was killed, but my two friends killed two Turkana. I attended their cleansing ceremonies ....

THE LEGEND OF 'GIVE ME AN ENEMY'

Karimojong violence takes the form of a series of raids and counter-raids, each explained with reference to the previous. No group or individual takes responsibility for starting the cycle of violence. Each aggression is justified as being revenge for earlier attacks.

A Karimojong legend, known as the legend of 'give me an enemy', tells how, somewhere in the Karimojong past, when Lokolmoi was the elder of all of Karamoja, the warriors petitioned him to allow them to go and mount a raid. At that time the Karimojong were a single united group. They lived in Nakadanya, where they had first settled. Lokolmoi would not hear of it, and refused to authorise the raid, but the warriors pressed him, and would not leave him alone for days on end.

When it became obvious to the old man that the warriors and their parents were determined, he let them go. But he refused to bless the raid.

After the raid, the young men returned with cattle, and tales of their victory and of the death of many of the enemy.

One of the cattle camps that the Karimojong youth had attacked contained some of Lokolmoi's own cattle, and in the process of the attack, Lokolmoi's own son Arion was killed by the Karimojong warriors. They also carried away Lokolmoi's own cattle and brought them back as part of the spoils of war.

When the warriors returned, their parents recognised Lokolmoi's cattle, and confirmed that Arion had been killed. Lokolmoi listened in silence, forbade his family from crying, and then cursed the Karimojong, saying that in view of what had happened they would now turn on each other and kill their own. In the eyes of the Karimojong, this curse persists today in the cycle of raiding and revenge.

Geoff Sayer

'I restored my father's herd, and three years later we were back to normal. I managed to marry my first wife. My clan made its livestock contribution towards my marriage, and since then I have not raided.'

In contrast, compare the experiences of a 20 year old Karimojong warrior: 'My mother was killed when collecting firewood and two weeks later I mobilised my five friends to accompany me for revenge. This was when I was 19 years old, and since that time I have not forgiven them. In that particular incident, I killed two women who were fetching water at the spring. The gap the enemy created cannot be filled, I know, but I have to punish them. In some situations I accompany my friends whenever they need my help. So far I have participated in seven raids. Whether ceremonies are performed or not, we are forced to do the same.'

Since time immemorial, cattle raiding has been part of the pastoral production system itself. Accepted as a legitimate and reasonable way of acquiring enough animals to pay brideprice, or of rebuilding cattle stocks after drought or theft has depleted them, the Karimojong developed ways to regulate such behaviour. A raid required a blessing from the elders, spiritual leaders were consulted, and the advice of 'forecasters' was sought. In the last 20 years, however, Karimojong society has experienced profound change, change that has transformed the cattle raiding between Karimojong as well as relations between the Karimojong and their agricultural neighbours. There is one single and identifiable cause of the change – the proliferation of automatic guns.

▼ A young Karimojong herder with his rifle

Crispin Hughes/Panos

Guns, guns, guns

Modern weaponry is redefining power and authority within Karimojong society. The balance that previously existed between elders, who were the decision-makers, and their sons, who implemented the decisions, has disappeared. Increasingly, their access to guns makes young warriors both decision-makers and implementers.

The dominance of 'gun culture' in Karamoja can be traced back to the sacking of Moroto barracks in 1979. Before then very few Karimojong had access to guns. The weapons of war that had been used for generations were the spear and the shield. This technology imposed its own limits on the scale of fighting and the consequences for the victims. A warrior could not carry more than two spears, and attacks had to take place at close range. In this way, fatalities were not so common.

With the fall of Idi Amin, government authority – always rather tenuous in Karamoja – disappeared along with his troops. They left the barracks in Moroto town unattended, and full of sophisticated weapons. The Karimojong took the lot. Since then they have ransacked the barracks a second time, during the turmoil of the mid-1980s.

The preferred weapon is the AK47. These are light and can be easily carried by warriors on foot. They are extremely effective, capable of discharging hundreds of bullets per minute, and they are cheap. In fact, they have never been cheaper. In July 2000, the price of a new model AK47 was just two cows, and bullets the equivalent of a few pence.

There is now a well-established trade in guns in Karamoja. The weapons are made in Eastern Europe, China, Korea, and other parts of the world, not in Uganda. Yet they are readily available, even in the most remote parts of Karamoja. The principal source of supply for years has been the armed factions fighting in southern Sudan, just across the border. In small trading centres and villages in the north of Karamoja, it is not uncommon to find Sudanese soldiers bringing donkey-loads of guns and ammunition in exchange for cattle and grain.

Impact of conflict on women

For men, fighting appears to offer the prospect of glory, heroism, and status. In war, however, there are always victims – and in Karamoja the victims of conflict are often women. The changing nature of warfare in Karamoja means that women do not enjoy the levels of respect and protection that existed just 30 years ago. Whereas raiding was once predominantly an event of the rangeland, now homesteads too are attacked, making women and children as vulnerable to attack as men. Although women take no physical part in raiding, they suffer directly when the other side comes for revenge. The militarisation of Karimojong society has been an entirely male phenomenon, and because women do not bear arms, they do not have the means to defend themselves. In addition, their isolation from wider Ugandan society means that Karimojong women are not benefiting from the social and political gains made by other Ugandan women as a result of progressive policies at national level. This does not mean that women do not share in the reflected glory of war. Women sing praises and celebrate when their warrior menfolk arrive with the spoils of war. By making comparisons

▼ *Karimojong women like Regina are excluded from the benefits of progress towards equality between men and women in Uganda.*

Geoff Sayer

▶ *The Karimojong 'buried the pen' because they felt threatened by schooling that was alien and undermining to their way of life.*

Geoff Sayer

that are intended to embarrass or shame, there is no doubt that women can exercise psychological pressure upon men to initiate or join a raid. However, in the words of Regina, 'My husband tries [to go cattle raiding]. I don't encourage it. I worry about the fighting. In these days you can easily lose your husband.... For me, a good husband is one who has respect from other people, but who doesn't go to raid.'

Burying the pen: placing a curse on modern education

The doubts of the Karimojong as to the objectives and benefits of modern schooling were so profound that, in 1940, a group of elders took action. In the sacred grove of their clan they performed a ceremony known as 'burying the pen'. The pen was seen as an instrument of oppression, a symbol of a way of life that the elders did not understand, and did not welcome. By burying the pen, a curse was put upon education so that it could no longer threaten traditional values.

Because of the Karimojong's lack of interest in education, and an equivalent lack of government investment, over 90 per cent of Karimojong children did not attend school in the early 1990s. Explanations for such low attendances may be derived from a critique of the education provided. School buildings are dilapidated, there are few trained teachers, and the relevance of the curriculum, taught in a language that few understand properly, has been questioned. An understanding of the role that children play in the household economy also helps to explain their lack of attendance. Amongst the Karimojong themselves, however, the chronic and almost complete marginalisation of education was understood to mean that the curse on education that was declared when the pen was buried was still effective.

WHY DON'T KARIMOJONG CHILDREN GO TO SCHOOL?

The most common reasons given by parents for their children not attending school revolve around children's role in the household economy. For Karimojong households, where everything is done by hand, labour is the most important element of production. Children work hard at home, and the benefits of schooling or any other daily activity

outside the home are weighed against the household's most basic labour needs. Girls work in and around the home, collecting water (which in semi-arid areas like Karamoja may take hours), grinding food, cultivating and weeding, cooking, and caring for younger children and the sick. Boys must acquire herding skills and knowledge of the rangeland environment at an early age if they are to look after the family herd. As one elder said, 'My boys have never gone to school. The cattle camp is their school.'

Since most parents have not been to school themselves, they find it hard to see what benefits education may bring. Over generations, this becomes a self-perpetuating process.

The reluctance of parents to send girls in particular to school is partly due to the Karimojong custom of brideprice. Traditionally when a girl marries, her family will receive wealth in the form of cattle from the new husband's family. In a society as poor as Karamoja, where assets are few and hunger is identified time and again by most people as their biggest problem, the value of having a girl who may bring 60 or even 100 cattle into the household when she is married is enormous. Parents fear that if their daughters go to school they will 'be spoilt', by which it is meant they will be less competent wives, because in school they do not learn the skills needed to run a household. Even worse, some parents worry that their daughters may meet a non-Karimojong man and never return to the traditional way of life.

Geoff Sayer

Unearthing the pen: the Karimojong bury the curse

As an indication of how attitudes were beginning to change, the generation following those who made the curse began to feel it was time to 'open up the way for the children'. They requested the elders to lift the curse so that their children might succeed at school, and thus lay the basis for advancing Karimojong interests economically, politically, and socially. With this in mind, the elders were requested to 'unearth the pen'. The unearthing ceremony took place in November 1995. The sons of the men who originally conducted the ceremony re-enacted their father's roles. Elders of all the clans present when the curse was imposed were represented, and appealed for it to be removed.

By unearthing the pen, the Karimojong elders have indicated their readiness to review decisions made long ago, and to begin to accept that change will happen, and that its benefits may be maximised if their children have access to education. As important as the ceremony itself were the preparations for it, and the role of the government. Notions that the Karimojong are simply irrational in their resistance to change were put aside as the government engaged in a consultation process which, in form and venue, was designed to suit the Karimojong themselves. The elders met with very senior government officials and explained their concerns. They asked, 'Why does the education that is given in schools make our children run away from our homes? Why does it make our children disrespectful to their parents and elders?' They asked why it was that

▲ ▼ *Peter Lowok practises his letters and numbers, and a young girl runs to the informal school. On her back she carries a baby sibling who will stay with her through class.*

Geoff Sayer

Geoff Sayer

when children leave primary school they appear to be lost and incapable of doing anything – unable to construct a house, look after animals, or even make a stool to sit on. They asked why there are so few schools in Karamoja that children have to travel long distances or even stay away from home in order to attend; they explained how for Karimojong parents this creates an unacceptable lack of contact with their children, and means they have little knowledge of what their children learn in school.

These questions were received in a spirit of critical feedback on the relevance and quality of education, and have led to the creation of a new project, Alternative Basic Eduation for Karamoja (ABEK).

A new beginning: alternative education in Karamoja

About 5km from Moroto town, and just a 100 yards or so from the homestead of Lorochom Lokoru, stands the shell of a small rectangular building. With only a frame of wooden posts held together by plaited, thin branches, it doesn't look much. It has no door and no roof, and is barely big enough for the 40 or so children who have squeezed into it.

Modest it may be, but this is school to Natule Munyes and her friends. Inside the half completed building, there is a deep silence, the silence of concentration and thought, as the children practice adding numbers. Natule completes her sums quickly and gets them all right, but she says that division is harder and gives her problems.

▼ *Alternative Basic Education for Karamoja (ABEK) schools may have few facilities, but they provide local, flexible, and appropriate learning environments for Karimojong children.*

Geoff Sayer

▶ *Natule gets her maths checked. More than 4000 children are learning in ABEK schools, and more than half of them are girls.*

▲ *Zacharia Lokorimoe teaches his class to read.*

Just behind Natule, another girl is busy looking after her little brother. He is not well, and has been crying. She has stopped doing her maths exercise to comfort him. In a formal primary school she would never have been allowed to bring her younger sibling into the classroom, but this is an ABEK Learning Centre and here the rules are different. ABEK is based on the premise that by making education accessible and relevant, parents and children alike will begin to appreciate the value of education and will respond positively to its availability. The facilitator at this learning centre, Zacharia Lokorimoe, says he thinks it is beginning to work. Zacharia is a tall, softly spoken man – unusual perhaps for someone who was in Uganda's Administration Police for more than 20 years. Zacharia lives on the edge of Moroto town some miles away, and walks to the learning centre twice a day to take his class. The responsibility for looking after all of the school's equipment and materials lies with the homestead, not with him. Zacharia moves on to another subject. The style is different this time, deliberately questioning, interactive, and participatory. The subject is drunkenness and the girls are as vigorous as the boys in speaking out and answering Zacharia's questions.

Meanwhile, a small boy briefly leaves the class. Beckoned by an older brother, he walks quickly across to the homestead and emerges a few minutes later with a small, thin stick in his right hand, gently encouraging a handful of goats to move through the gateway of the homestead. His job done, the little boy returns to his class while his brother and the goats head off for another day on the range.

Economy and livelihoods

A small, agricultural economy

Colonialism had a profound effect on Uganda's economy and on the livelihoods of its people. Uganda was integrated into a trading system that was shaped to meet the interests of an elite in Britain. Uganda's role was to produce particular commodities – notably cotton at first, then coffee – and to do so by means of millions of small-holders who provided for their own subsistence through the cultivation of food crops, such as millet, bananas, cassava, and sweet potatoes. Attempts to introduce large-scale crop plantations were not economically viable. Today, sugar-cane estates between Kampala and Jinja are the principal vestiges of the attempt to create a plantation economy in Uganda.

Since the colonial days, little has changed in the relative importance of the agricultural, industrial, and other sectors of Uganda's economy. No longer integrated into an imperial trading system, Uganda has now been incorporated into a global market. Otherwise, the role of Uganda's producers is pretty much the same as it has been for generations.

Agriculture remains by far the most important sector of the economy. This creates a trade pattern of exports dominated by agricultural products, and imports dominated by manufactured goods. The economy is heavily dependent on coffee, which accounts for some 55 per cent of export earnings. Coffee prices, like those of many agricultural commodities, are extremely volatile. When the coffee harvest is good and the international price of coffee is high, Uganda's export earnings increase. When the world coffee price drops, the value of its exports will plummet accordingly. This means that gains achieved through painfully negotiated debt relief may be almost wiped out by a fall in export earnings resulting from a decrease in the price of a single commodity.

▼ Kakira sugar estate is one of the last remaining examples of large-scale crop plantations in Uganda.

Geoff Sayer

Geoff Sayer

▲ ▼ *Most agriculture in Uganda is small-scale and family-based. Many children, like Priscilla and Pennina hoeing pineapples below, work hard on the family farm as well as going to school.*

Geoff Sayer

Uganda will always be vulnerable to changes in world commodity prices because it has no influence on their level. It has so little influence because it is such a small economy, producing commodities that many other countries also produce. Uganda's annual export earnings total only around 600 million US dollars, less than one-thousandth of the size of US export earnings.

Uganda's dependence on agricultural commodities means that the rural economy, not the urban economy, is the most important in terms of national wealth and individual wellbeing. A small rural economy also means that most Ugandans still rely almost entirely on their own and family labour – they collect water by hand, gather firewood by hand, dig by hand, and harvest by hand. Only about five per cent of the Ugandan population have regular access to electricity – even many urban dwellers rely on kerosene lamps – and about 90 per cent of Uganda's total energy requirements are met using firewood and charcoal.

The fact that so much agricultural work is carried out on a small scale by unpaid family workers means that a significant sector of the economy is classified as 'non-monetary'. Indeed, for many Ugandans, the concept of 'the market' is a distant one. People's first priority is to meet their survival needs. Their resilience in doing so – despite political, military, or economic turmoil – has been both impressive and lifesaving.

Uneven economic development

Colonialism built upon differences in economic development apparent in pre-colonial times in such a way as to produce a strongly unbalanced economy. As a result, disparities in income between the 'fertile crescent' around Lake Victoria and the poorer, drier northern districts became pronounced. With the construction of the railway from Mombasa to Kampala in the early 1900s, which effectively incorporated southern Uganda into the imperial economy, areas with reasonable access to the railway were encouraged to produce cotton for export to Britain. Cultivation expanded rapidly, but in an economy which was still totally dependent on

► *World coffee prices fluctuate constantly – spelling insecurity for small farmers like Molly Nantongo.*

hand labour, a critical factor in the successful introduction of new crops was the provision of an adequate labour supply. This demand was partly met by the smallholders of Buganda and Busoga, the principal producers of cotton, and partly by employing migrant workers from the economically peripheral areas of the country. Coffee, too, was introduced, and so extensive was its adoption that it gradually replaced cotton as the principal cash crop of the south.

Uneven agricultural development has been reinforced by patterns of industrial and manufacturing development. The industrial heartland of Uganda, such as it is, spreads from Jinja in the east to Masaka in the west. Apart from the exceptional 'prestige project', such as the Lira Textile Mill in northern Uganda, there has been little attempt to modernise the structure of the economy in the areas beyond 'the crescent'. It is an imbalance that the subsequent growth in commerce, public administration, and services has only exacerbated.

A consequence of this uneven distribution of opportunities was a division of labour based on geography, but dangerously open to interpretations based on ethnicity. People living in the 'fertile crescent' around Lake Victoria would grow cash crops, while the people of northern and south-western Uganda provided these crop farmers with a supply of migrant workers. Formalising this division, the colonial authorities designated northern and south-western Uganda as labour reserves rather than production zones.

Even more important for the future of Uganda, the colonial state dealt with the resulting disparities in development between the north and south by recruiting most of the men it needed for the army and the police force from northern districts. The same situation has prevailed since independence, with the relative poverty and lack of opportunities in the

▲ *Depending for their raw materials on local agriculture, breweries are among the most profitable industries in East Africa.*

▼ *Pius Beingana makes iron window frames at the roadside plot that is his factory and shop. The informal sector is thriving in Uganda, where entrepreneurs build successful local businesses with the smallest of capital investments.*

north impelling young men to join the army. The unbalanced composition of the army has made it open to abuse by politicians and military leaders who put their personal and ethnic interests above national ones.

The process of uneven development meant that by the mid-1950s, farmers in Buganda had cash incomes higher than anywhere else in the country – three times those of farmers in Acholi and West Nile, and nine times higher than the cattle herders of Karamoja. The relative prosperity of southern Uganda was inextricably tied to the marginalisation of the north and the south-west. Today, however, whereas parts of south-western Uganda, such as Ankole, have benefited from relative peace and security and from investments in infrastructure, the northern districts have suffered prolonged insecurity of a kind which has impoverished the citizens of those districts and has created little incentive for private investment and little opportunity for public investment in roads, power supplies, and telecommunications.

Regional imbalances in Uganda's economy are not new. They have existed since pre-colonial times and are a result of a complex intermingling of history, geography, climate, and agricultural development as well as policy directives from successive governments since the creation of Uganda a century ago. Neither the first Obote government of 1962-71, nor Amin's regime, significantly redressed these imbalances, despite the fact that both leaders were northerners. On the contrary, their economic policies only served to further impoverish and marginalise the north. Post-independence governments of all kinds have been confronted with the negative consequences of regional disparities. Collectively, they have failed to use economic development as a means of promoting equity and consolidating nationhood, as well as a means of achieving sustainable growth.

Growth and aid

Aside from these regional disparities, until 1971 the national economy had been reasonably well-managed. However, the years of Idi Amin and Obote II were disastrous. Hyperinflation meant price increases of as much as 200 per cent per year, and the most basic and essential commodities, like soap, sugar, and salt, were scarce. Black marketeering and smuggling undermined normal trade patterns. Wages became increasingly worthless, and there were corresponding increases in petty corruption. The impact of these years on the structure of the economy signified the start of a process that produced sharper and sharper contrasts between private wealth and public decay, while the collapse of the formal sector led to the emergence and strengthening of an informal sector. The informal sector now dominates the Ugandan economy, both in terms of the numbers of people who are involved in informal economic activity, and the value of this activity to the national economy.

MALWA AND MATOOKE – FOOD AND DRINK IN UGANDA'S INFORMAL ECONOMY

In Uganda, the formal sector drinks industry is dominated by big companies, huge bottling plants, and new breweries. Expanding, it is one of Uganda's major employers, and a significant contributor to the national economy. Less visible, and operating in a completely different way, is a community-level brewing industry.

Malwa is a traditional millet beer, originating in Teso, north-east Uganda, and now an extremely popular drink in most parts of the country. Malwa brewing is a vibrant and expanding element of the informal brewing industry. It is dominated by women, tens of thousands of whom earn their living in this way. Instead of using sophisticated machinery to produce a standard product, malwa is a genuine 'home brew', and all stages of production are done entirely by hand. The taste will vary according to the quantity and quality of the ingredients, and the skill of the brewer.

If malwa is the national drink of Uganda, matooke, or cooked bananas, can reasonably claim to be the national food. Bananas are something special in Uganda. They grow best in the damper climate and richer soils of southern and western Uganda, or on the slopes of the mountains. Uganda produces millions of bananas every year. Most of them are green bananas that can be boiled, steamed, roasted on charcoal, or, as a replacement for millet, used in the local manufacture of beer. With so many uses, there are lots of different varieties.

Early in the morning, a common sight is a yellow Tata lorry, packed with hundreds of neatly stacked bunches of bananas. Bunches may be a metre long and weigh up to 20 kg. These lorries trundle their way up the tarmac road from the west to Kampala, where the demand for bananas is insatiable. In every part of Kampala there are small markets, each one served direct by these lorries. One of them is Kansanga.

As the lorries arrive, young men gather in the growing light of the dawn to help unload. All of the purchasers are women, who supervise the men's work. The melée of activity may look chaotic, but in fact it is highly organised. Each line of bananas, stretching from the edge of the pavement to a line of wooden kiosks a few yards behind, belongs to an individual woman. And within that line the bananas are stacked in rows according to their size and price. As a young man places another huge bunch on the ground, he breaks off two bananas and places them in a little pile at the back of the pavement. This is his payment – he gets no money, but is allowed to take two bananas from each bunch. At the end of the morning he will take his pickings, and sell them. As soon as the delivery is completed, the purchaser sits down on the pavement and starts to peel some of the bananas she has just bought. She works quickly, and soon a pile of banana skins, green on the outside and almost white inside, builds upon the ground. These peelings will be saved – mounds of them are a common sight near markets or outside cooking places – because they can be used or sold as feed for cows.

TODAY'S MENU
MATOOKE+MEAT 1000=
HALF-MATOOKE 700=
MATOOKE+FISH 100=
MATOOKE+POSHO 1000=
MATOOKE+BEANS 700=
MATOOKE+G.NUTS 700=
SAMOSA 200=

Geoff Sayer

Geoff Sayer

A remarkable economic recovery...

It is against this background that the achievements of the current government need to be understood. Recognising that Uganda had no choice but to seek external financial assistance, the NRM buried its initial economic strategy, which was designed to overcome the colonial legacy of 'producing what we do not consume, and consuming what we do not produce', and embraced the policies of economic orthodoxy. However reluctant it was at first, the government has persisted with that strategy, and now has a long and impressive record of 'financial discipline and economic competence' which is acknowledged internationally and is reflected in an uninterrupted series of arrangements with the International Monetary Fund (IMF) stretching back to 1987. By any standard, the achievements of the last ten years or so are impressive. The Ugandan economy has experienced consistently positive growth rates of between 5–10 per cent, low annual inflation (less than ten per cent), and a currency with a reasonably stable exchange rate backed by steadily increasing foreign exchange reserves.

Uganda's remarkable economic recovery has been based on the scale and consistency of foreign aid the country receives. In 1986, the year the NRM came to power, official development assistance amounted to approximately US$200 million. By 1997, as a result of close working relationships built up between the government and the international financial institutions and donors, aid from the IMF, the World Bank, and donor governments had increased to nearly US$850 million.

These ever-increasing injections of foreign aid have been essential for the long-term rehabilitation of infrastructure, for funding new projects, and for balance of payments support. Indeed, the size of the trade balance is an indication of the extent to which Uganda has succeeded in attracting donor assistance to fund its import bill. The gap between imports and exports has grown steadily since the mid-1980s: while exports have increased only modestly, imports have mushroomed. In 1998–9, their value was over US$1.3 billion, with the proportion covered by export income having declined from 70 per cent in 1987 to just 40 per cent.

▼ At Jinja market, Ugandan rice sells for the same price as rice from Pakistan and Vietnam. Liberalisation means that cheap imports can undermine prices for local goods.

Geoff Sayer

... but dependency and poverty remain

The irony of Uganda's recovery is that the macroeconomic stability that has been achieved is based almost entirely on concessional, and conditional, transfers of development aid, and not on any fundamental improvement in the basic structure or capacity of the economy. Uganda is completely dependent on aid, and while dependency continues, so does poverty.

BODABODA BOYS

On the edge of almost any town market in Uganda there will be a dozen or more young men standing by their bicycles, their eyes constantly flicking across the busy scene in front of them as they look for potential customers. The bicycle is the essential small business vehicle of Uganda, where it has even become a taxi. The bikes of these bodaboda boys, as they are called, are distinctive for their decoration

with brightly coloured woven trim, and red, green, or orange tassels. On the front they carry a metal registration number plate, issued by the local Bodaboda Association. On the back is a padded seat for customers. On the frames of the bikes, stickers announce 'No Money, No Life' or 'No-one but Jesus'. Not all the young men can afford to buy a bicycle, which costs £50 or more, and many will rent one for the day instead.

Bodaboda boys epitomise the imagination and opportunism of the informal economy. They first appeared during the 1980s in towns close to the Kenyan border. At that time, the border was sometimes closed, and the movement of goods across it became difficult and time-consuming. To get around these problems, young men started stacking all kinds of commodities on the back of their bikes, and using small tracks to cross the border. Because they moved from one border to another, so they became known as 'bodaboda'.

Uganda has followed its agreements with the IMF scrupulously; it has adhered to the innumerable conditions set over the years; it has devoted huge efforts to negotiations with donors and banks; and it has made extremely clever use of technical assistance, particularly in relation to seeking debt relief. Despite all of this, Uganda remains one of the poorest, least developed, and highly indebted countries in the world today. Of a total of 174 countries in the United Nations Development Programme Human Development Index, Uganda is ranked 158th.

Uganda's economic revival demonstrates that growth does not necessarily lead to poverty reduction. Poverty reduction depends on how the benefits of growth are distributed and utilised. The most obvious consequence of recent economic growth is in the associated growth of inequality.

Benefits for the few

In Uganda, there is an emerging elite, increasingly well-off and sophisticated, and urban and commercial in character. Kampala has enjoyed a property boom for years. On the rolling hillsides that characterise the city and its outskirts, increasingly splendid houses symbolise 'new wealth'. In Uganda, such investments in property are still made by individuals, not by building societies or banks, and a businessman or a government official may have five, ten, or more houses to rent out to members of the business and expatriate communities. This elite has enough money, connections, and access to information to benefit from economic growth. It is also well-placed to enjoy the fruits of Uganda's shift to a market economy, in which state companies are sold off to private bidders, and where links with foreign investors and companies are beneficial.

Meanwhile, a section of the Ugandan population has got poorer, not richer, over the last 15 years. Most at risk of increased poverty and vulnerability have been those small-scale peasant producers trying to eke out a living in areas where conflict and insecurity have become a way of life.

The majority of Uganda's citizens live between these two extremes. They continue to have very low cash incomes, grow much of their own food, and struggle to meet the costs of any unexpected emergency. These people may not feel part of 'an inspirational success story', but they are beginning to benefit – for the first time

▼ Houses for the wealthy elite, under construction in Kampala

Geoff Sayer

in decades – from a government committed to increasing the incomes of the poor and to improving their quality of life through the universal provision of basic social services.

Finding the money for health care

Uganda's infant mortality rate and life expectancy are among the worst in the world. More than 50 per cent of Ugandans have no access to clean water, making them vulnerable to cholera and diarrhoea. Malaria and respiratory illnesses are widespread, and a frequent cause of death. Yet many of these common illnesses can be prevented or easily treated.

The Ugandan government struggles to provide adequate health care to its population. Health care provision and infrastructure in Uganda are chronically underfunded and highly variable in quality. A system of 'cost sharing', whereby hospitals must charge for treatments, means that most Ugandans have to pay for health care when they get sick. In many places, an important role in health care provision is undertaken by private hospitals, like the Kagando Mission Hospital in western Uganda. Although private hospitals receive some funding from the government, this can be erratic, and hospitals must generate other income by charging patients for services. In general, government hospitals are better funded, but they too are required to charge for their services.

Hospital staff describe how they struggle to avoid passing the financial pressures on to their patients, 'The money is difficult for them to find,' said Sister Annette Namatovu. 'Of course, if they come and tell us they have no money, that they cannot pay, we will accept that.'

▼ Nursing sister Annette Namatovu talks to Astrida Kabugho in the children's ward at Kagando Hospital, where Astrida's daughter Nancy is being treated for malaria. Astrida has to consider how she will meet the cost. 'We can't easily pay. To pay the fees people will sell a goat or a pig, even a bike or a radio. But the first thing is to get treatment.'

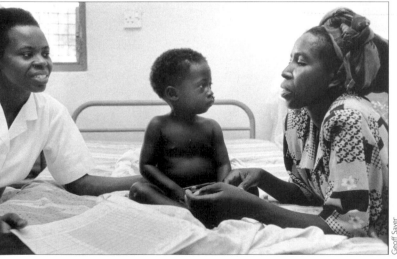
Geoff Sayer

The cost of health care means that many Ugandans turn to cheaper traditional medicines before they will attend a hospital. It also means that people with illnesses will often delay for as long as possible before seeking treatment. As Astrida Kabugho explains, 'When a child is ill, parents often stay at home and wait. They hope the malaria will not be strong. It's not easy to watch your child sicken, and wonder whether you should go now, or wait another day.' Illnesses that would be easily treatable in the early stages, like malaria, become more serious as they progress. Delays in seeking treatment can result in increased hospital expenses, serious illness, or even death for some patients.

A recent government initiative to extend the access and quality of local health care is beginning to tackle some of these problems. The creation of 'health sub-districts', administered by local hospitals, has underpinned the formation of a network of community health services. Local health services, which were moribund in the early 1990s, are now better-resourced, and provide rural Ugandans with an alternative to travelling to hospitals for minor illnesses and maternity care. They also have an important role in public health education, through specially trained community health workers. Astrida explains, 'The community health workers in the village advise us about immunisation, how to prevent illnesses such as cholera, and what to do if children become ill with diarrhoea or a fever.' John Kaahwa tells how, 'There have been big changes in the behaviour, and in the health of the community. People drink clean water now, and realise why they should. All the children are immunised.'

Policies to eradicate poverty

By the mid-1990s, ten years after the first agreement with the IMF, the Ugandan government and its principal donors recognised that the benefits of growth were not reaching the poorest Ugandans. Recognising that economic growth will be sustainable only if it addresses the needs of the vast majority of its citizens, the government declared that poverty reduction was the overall goal of its economic policy. A Poverty Eradication Plan was approved in 1997, designed to wipe out poverty within 20 years. Preparatory work for the plan confirmed the scale of the problem – over 66 per cent of Ugandans were found to be living below the poverty line, on less than US$15 per month. The Plan stresses the need to increase the incomes of poor men and women, and the importance of providing good quality, publicly funded social services. The latter are especially critical in an economy that is still largely subsistence-based, not cash-based. If education, health, and social services are only available on payment of cash, this effectively denies access to those services to those who have very small cash incomes – often the very people who can benefit most from the provision of services. For this reason, poor people themselves have complained bitterly about the impact of school fees and health charges. It is perhaps no coincidence that the adoption of an explicit Poverty Eradication Policy was accompanied by the introduction of universal primary education.

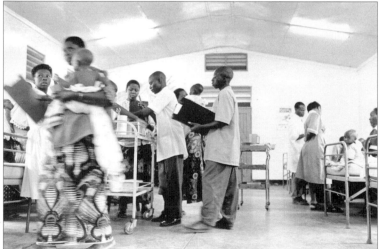

▼ Kagando Hospital does not turn poor patients away, even when they have no money to pay for care. Instead of fees, patients and their relatives often pay in kind, leaving radios, clothes, blankets, pots and pans, even goats and cows. When enough has accumulated, the hospital holds a sale.

Geoff Sayer

Education

Geoff Sayer

▲ *Since universal primary education was introduced in 1997, Dorothy Policeapuuli has seen enrolments double in her school.*

▼ *Phoebe picks the cotton that will pay for her schooling. Her father John Kaahwa was determined that all his children should be educated, whatever the cost. Phoebe has now become a nurse.*

Geoff Sayer

Before universal primary education

Kinyamaseke Primary School is a typical rural school in the Kasese district of western Uganda. Back in 1993, Dorothy Policeapuuli, the deputy head teacher, described the difficulties her staff and pupils were facing. 'We have only 438 pupils enrolled this year compared with 560 in 1992. Fees have risen out of all proportion during the past few years. Children are dropping out because their parents can't afford the fees. But we can't manage without the income. We have to send children home or parents won't pay ... but sometimes the children just don't return.'

At the same time, John Kaahwa expressed the frustrations of millions of parents. 'We grow almost all our own food. We buy meat once a week ... other than that we have to buy a few essentials – clothes, shoes, soap, salt, and sugar. We have to pay the government tax – but the biggest expense is school fees. We are struggling now for such a small profit it seems hopeless, to work so hard and fail even to keep the children at school. We are working for nothing. You can see my children, they're here – sent back from school. I haven't paid for this term and the school isn't prepared to wait. The children are sent home so I go to kneel down and promise payment. Then they are allowed back for a few days before being sent home again.'

By the mid-1990s, parents across Uganda were struggling to pay school fees, the largest recurrent household expense for many families. The costs of education were equivalent to about one-fifth of the annual income of an average Ugandan family. As a result, almost one-third of school-age Ugandan children were not enrolled in school at all. Of the children who enrolled in primary school, very few were likely to progress all the way through to the final grade: faced with rising fees, many children were not able to complete their education. Overall, the government's spending on education amounted to just 1.6 per cent of GDP.

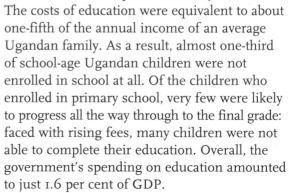

Universal primary education – a catalyst for change

In 1997 the Ugandan government made the decision to provide free primary education for four children from every family. This is part of a strategy aimed at achieving universal primary education (UPE) in Uganda by 2003. Ambitious goals set for 2003 include the construction of 25,000 classrooms, the provision of a free set of textbooks for all children, and improvements to teacher training. Public spending on education has risen to some four per cent of GDP, with primary-level education accounting for two-thirds of this.

The impact of the decision has been enormous and immediate. The number of pupils attending primary schools doubled almost overnight, with enrolments rising from 2.6 million in 1996 to 5.1 million in 1997.

At the end of 1996, 662 pupils were attending Kinyamaseke Primary School. In January 1997 the school reopened its doors to 1211 pupils. Dazed teachers had to work out how to accommodate 471 pupils in primary 1 classes alone, and more than 100 new pupils in primary 2.

'Of course it was a shock – it was chaos!' recalls head teacher Patrick Bwambale. 'Here in Kinyamaseke, we were a little prepared and in 1997 the teachers in years 1 and 2 had classes of 110, while we kept the class size in years 3-7 below 55. Teachers were anxious about the heavy enrolment. Some were afraid that the whole venture would fail. Now we are relieved: according to what we see in our school, and the other schools around, we have hope that our work will be successful. Things are getting better, and more children have the benefit of education.'

As Patrick spoke, builders were busy outside his office. Two new classrooms were being constructed, thanks to a grant provided from the government's Poverty Action Fund. Patrick also described efforts to develop a new curriculum that will be responsive to the needs of Ugandan communities.

Geoff Sayer

▲ *Aisa and Christine (left) pore over their new textbooks at Kinyamaseke school.*

Geoff Sayer

'A new curriculum has been introduced. For the first three years, the medium of teaching is now the mother tongue [instead of English]. This is a good change for the pupil. The new curriculum reflects the local environment. There are also new subjects – Swahili, agriculture, and community services. Another new subject is population and family life education. This will deal with reproduction, family spacing, hygiene, and health, previously covered only as part of science. The new curriculum is also encouraging group work amongst children. If you have a class of 100, you can't do it. But class sizes are coming down, and this kind of teaching will come into play.'

The drive towards universal primary education demonstrates the Ugandan government's real commitment to placing education at the heart of strategies to eradicate poverty. It shows, too, that political will can be as important as income in determining a country's capacity to provide basic services. Most importantly of all, the introduction of universal primary education has given millions of teachers, parents, and pupils new hope for the future and the opportunities it may hold.

Beyond the basics – extending educational reform

The government's commitment to educational reform is not confined to primary education. While spending on primary education is taking the largest slice of the new funding, education at secondary and university levels is also being transformed.

The 2003 educational targets include the aim that 65 per cent of children should make the transition from primary school to more advanced education in secondary schools. Currently, only about 40 per cent of primary school leavers do so. Investment at secondary school level in Uganda has led to marked increases in the numbers of secondary schools in the country, and the number of enrolments. In 1994 there were 557 secondary schools with around 180,000 students enrolled. Today, around half a million students attend some 837 secondary schools across Uganda. However, much of the growth in new schools is in the private sector.

Increased numbers of secondary schools, combined with their spread into more rural areas of the country, have helped to increase access to this level of schooling. However, attendance at secondary school in Uganda

Faith Muhindo Thembo (right) prepares a teaching schedule with friends Justine, Escovia, and Rosemary at Bwera Teacher Training College. The introduction of UPE has improved teachers' salaries and career paths. For Faith and her colleagues, teaching in the 21st century should bring exciting challenges.

Geoff Sayer

costs money, for fees, and for books and stationery. Although some bursaries exist for poor children, fees remain a major determinant of access to advanced education for the majority of Ugandans. In addition, there are major disparities in facilities and exam performance between the government-funded and private schools. The availability of universal primary education is creating new cohorts of children leaving primary school with high expectations for the future. To fulfil their hopes and expectations, and to build on the successes of UPE, it is crucial that the Ugandan government creates credible ways of giving these young people access to good quality secondary education.

▼ Simon is helped into his classroom by a friend. Since the introduction of UPE, many more disabled children have made their way to school. Now, the challenge for the government is to develop teaching for pupils with sight, speech, hearing, and mental impairment.

Geoff Sayer

Makerere

In 1922 the colonial authorities established a technical school on Makerere Hill in Kampala. It had just 14 students. During the next decade the school became a college, it offered a broader range of courses, and the vision that Makerere College should become a centre of higher education was developed. In 1949 it became Makerere University College, affiliated initially to the University of London, and later becoming part of the University of East Africa. It was designed to produce an African intelligentsia.

When Idi Amin took power, clouds began to gather over Makerere. The politics of fear and favouritism took root there as they did elsewhere in the country, with students informing on colleagues and lecturers.

Geoff Sayer

▲ Fees may mean the lawns and grand architecture at Makerere become increasingly the preserve of a wealthy elite.

Staff began to leave under the pressure, the support of major donors and educational foundations dried up, and the physical infrastructure of the University started to fall into disrepair. Makerere became an under-funded, dilapidated university offering degrees of questionable quality.

The situation improved through the 1990s, to the point where Makerere aspires to become again East Africa's pre-eminent institute of higher learning. New courses have been introduced and the campus facilities have been renovated and expanded. The driving force behind these changes is the adoption of a financing strategy based on private funding to complement government support. Ten years ago, Makerere had fewer than 5000 students, almost all of them government-sponsored. Today, the University has over 20,000 students enrolled. At least 75 per cent of these students are fee-paying. Critics see this as the privatisation of higher education and condemn its potential to make university education primarily available only to the elite and the growing middle class. To others, the progress of the last ten years is not only a source of pride and satisfaction, it is also a pragmatic acceptance of the fact that, in the context of severely limited state funding, alternative approaches had to be tried.

The current emphasis on primary education is a crucial starting-point for educational reform in Uganda. It is an important recognition of the potential of education to reduce poverty and extend opportunities for all. At the same time, some Ugandans fear that the value of publicly funded higher education may be overlooked, with access increasingly restricted to the wealthy. Uganda needs individuals, groups, and organisations with the capacity to analyse, express alternative opinions, and organise for effective engagement with government. It is no coincidence that the best of the thousands of community groups and national organisations that have appeared in the last 10-15 years have largely been created by people who combine the benefits of higher education with a commitment to addressing social injustice and poverty.

Politics and freedoms

In 1986, Uganda's democratic pedigree was non-existent. The constitution had been altered and disregarded. Local government had been systematically downgraded and made dependent on central government power and patronage. The coercive power of the state had been used against its own citizens to such an extent that it represented the biggest threat to their safety and prosperity.

The National Resistance Movement (NRM) describes itself as a 'no-party, mass movement democracy'. It came to power proclaiming that it represented a fundamental shift in the politics of Uganda, and with the clear intention of reshaping the role of the state and of ending 'bad governance'. Determined to redress the injustices and abuses that had characterised earlier governments and regimes, the NRM developed a programme to restore democracy and consolidate national unity.

The yellow bus was adopted as the symbol of the National Resistance Movement before the referendum held in June 2000.

Geoff Sayer

Ending sectarian politics

The NRM – or Movement as it is now more commonly known – was designed in response to an analysis of Uganda's troubles that highlighted the damage done by sectarian politics. In Uganda, 'sectarian' means divisions based on religious or ethnic differences. Uganda is not divided into classes in the same way that European society was when its existing political systems were being shaped. Whilst a party-based political system may be appropriate as a way of expressing 'the class struggle', the fact that the vast majority of Ugandans are small-scale farmers means that they have the same economic interests, irrespective of tribe or religion. Because economic interests are widely shared, political parties have tended to form along the lines of other, sectarian, divisions. The Movement describes itself as a 'political system [that] brings people of different shades of opinion and identities to

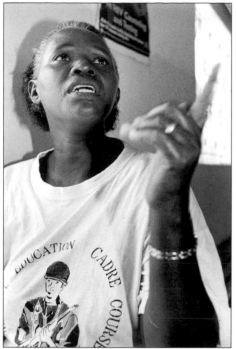

▲ *The Movement system has been instrumental in promoting the inclusion of women in politics. Today, Uganda boasts a vocal and influential women's movement, and a parliamentary seat from each of the 39 districts is reserved for women.*

Geoff Sayer

work together in order to develop their country. The movement is broad based, inclusive, non-partisan, non-sectarian, and committed to the principle of participatory democracy.'

'Individual merit'

If party-based politics would perpetuate intolerance and division, the challenge for Ugandans was to find a system that would promote participation, enforce accountability, and express democracy. The answer was to acknowledge the fundamental right of association, according to which political parties have the right to exist and individuals have the right to join them. In Uganda, however, political parties are not allowed to contest elections: only individuals can exercise that right. Candidates in any election – local, parliamentary, or presidential – stand on the basis of what is called 'individual merit', and not as a candidate for – or as a member of – a political party.

Individual merit, it is argued, allows people of a wide range of political opinions to contest elections. The electorate should be guided by the capacity and integrity of the individual, rather than voting for the party in whose name a candidate may be standing.

In principle, under the Movement system members of parliament can debate issues on the basis of their opinions and those of the people they represent, and not under the influence of party leadership. In practice, of course, the leadership of the Movement, like any government, exerts considerable influence over the behaviour of MPs.

In addition to representation through the direct election of constituency MPs or councillors, the Movement system also contains provisions for other groups of people to have their own representatives. This is intended to promote the inclusion of groups of people who were traditionally excluded from power and political office, in particular women, young people, and people with disabilities. These provisions have also been used to promote a sense of responsibility amongst those who sometimes abused their power in the past. For example, the army has been given representation in parliament as a way of incorporating it into constitutional politics.

There are criticisms of this system of political organization. The 'individual merit' system is alleged to be biased towards individuals with considerable financial resources and good connections. To many Ugandans, MPs are an unrepresentative elite motivated by personal ambition and benefits, rather than by a commitment to serve their community.

Critics of the NRM also argue that its no-party democracy is just a mask for a one-party state, and that the Movement is a political party by another name. Advocates of the Movement reject these criticisms by emphasising that NRM governments have consistently included individuals, up to the level of ministers, who were members of a range of political parties. In all elections, candidates are free to state their political convictions, including whether they are pro- or anti-Movement. This, the advocates argue, is clear proof that a system has been formed, and not a party in disguise.

The inadequacy of this division was exposed in the presidential elections, held in March 2001. The leading challenger, Colonel Kizza Besigye, came from within the Movement, was an old friend of the President, and an experienced soldier – characteristics that made him a serious contender. The emergence of a rival candidate from within the Movement was a big surprise. It demonstrates beyond doubt the current political dominance of the NRM, but lends weight to the argument that the Movement is not just a party without a name.

If the election was unique because the two leading contenders came from one political stable, it was regrettably reminiscent of earlier elections in other ways. For the first time since the NRM came to power, political violence marred the campaign. There were claims of harassment, intimidation, and rigging on both sides. The profile of the army raised anxieties about its role and impartiality. These features of the contest will have damaged the government's democratic credentials.

President Museveni won the election and was re-elected for another term. The election itself was a victory for the political maturity and restraint of Ugandans and, in particular, of Uganda's media. The extent of media coverage and the frankness of the reporting were balanced by a well-developed sense of responsibility that on occasion seemed to surpass that of some of the politicians involved.

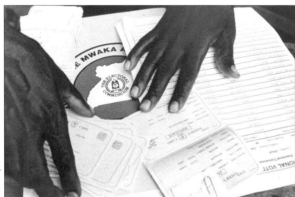

Geoff Sayer

▲ Voter registration cards being checked against the electoral list in Kitgum, northern Uganda, where dissatisfaction with the Movement means low turnouts at election time.

The referendum

The Movement has survived for nearly 15 years. This makes it by far the most durable political system that independent Uganda has ever had. However, the question of whether to adopt a consitution based on multi-party politics, or whether to continue with the Movement system, has remained a constant topic of debate. In June 2000 the question was put to the electorate in a referendum.

On the face of it, the results of the referendum were overwhelming. More than 90 per cent of voters affirmed the Movement system. However, the referendum also revealed a low voter turnout. Even in cities like Kampala where rallies and media debates were held daily in the run-up to the referendum, only about 50 per cent of the electorate voted. In northern

▲ *Saidi Kikoye posts his ballot paper at Kisasizi voting station in the Ugandan national referendum, June 2000.*

districts such as Kitgum and Gulu, the referendum was either boycotted, or, more commonly, considered to be irrelevant, and turnout was as low as ten per cent. For the Movement, which has based its legitimacy on its commitment to inclusion and participation, such low levels of engagement challenge the ethical foundations of its existence.

After decades in which the state, through its army, police, and security forces, has often waged war on its own people, it is not surprising that most Ugandans, and particularly those in the more prosperous and more peaceful south, should opt for the status quo. But pressures from within, and from external donor governments, are likely eventually to bring multi-partyism to Uganda.

This will have both positive and negative effects. The way in which the Movement has created the 'space' for marginalised groups with little previous experience of political organisation or representation to participate in national life is widely judged to have been a progressive and successful measure. A return to a simple multi-party system, based on a single chamber of parliament, is not likely to be able to preserve this advance. Similarly, most Ugandans think that one of the biggest and most positive changes in politics in recent years has been the declining influence of religion. In the future, a critical issue will be the nature of the relationship between the churches and political parties.

The referendum did not provide a definitive answer to a question that has split political opinion in Uganda for the last decade. The result underlines the need for an extensive and open debate about the most appropriate political system for the country. Until now the choice has tended to be presented in stark and polarised terms that neither do justice to the importance of the issue, nor to the complexity of people's views.

From resistance councils to local councils

Among the most far-reaching and radical changes to take place in Ugandan politics since 1986 have been the transformations in local government. Before 1986, local government was under central control, with government ministers at liberty to confirm or withhold councillor appointments, or even to dismiss an entire local council.

When the NRM was fighting the 'bush war' in the early 1980s it created a new administrative system in the areas it controlled. This became known as the Resistance Council (RC) system. This was a five-tiered system ranging from the RC1 at village level, up to the RC5, which was the district council. Every adult man or woman became a member of the RC1 by virtue of their residence in the village, and elected a village resistance committee to manage their affairs. The members of all the RC1s in a parish then elected nine of their members to form the RC2, or parish council, and so on up to RC5.

The RC system has, over time, earned the confidence of most Ugandans and grown to be nationwide in scope. Because local representatives are elected, not appointed, under the RC system, local politicians are accountable to the people who elected them, instead of owing their allegiance to a central government. As simple as they may sound, these basic changes have transformed the image, power, status, and accountability of local government.

The effective establishment of the Resistance Councils was the precursor of radical reforms to decentralise local government. Under the decentralisation policy, Resistance Councils became Local Councils (LCs). The multi-tiered system below district level was preserved with few changes, but the radical change was to transfer significant functions, decision-making powers, staff, and resources from national ministries to local councils. Although there continue to be complaints of corruption, incompetence, or, more often, of insufficient technical and professional capacity, there is nevertheless an almost unanimous view that accountability has been enhanced, local knowledge and control have been increased, and, most critically, that local services have been improved under the new system.

John Kaahwa explained, 'At least with the LCs, we see that Museveni has done something for us. We are seeing benefits from the money that is collected from us in taxes. It is being used to develop the parish and sub-county, and we can see how it is being spent, we can feel the benefit.

Decentralisation is a good thing. Recently we had a problem with the Chairman of the LC3. We questioned him – we can do that. We know him, and we can find out what is going on. The LC system has empowered us. It has given us the right to ask questions and the means to ask questions.

'The LC1 coordinates activities in the parish. For example, we have been lacking water in my area, but we have organised ourselves through the LC to dig trenches and bring water nearer. Our LC is active in advising farmers to grow more food rather than cash crops. And when there is a dispute it is referred to the LC, and people accept the LC's judgement. If people don't agree, then they have the right to take it to the LC3 or to a court of law.'

▼ *Statue of Ronald Muwenda Mutebi II, 36th and current Kabaka of Buganda*

Geoff Sayer

Politics and identity

One of the most persistent and complex issues to shape Ugandan politics over the years has been the tension between tribal and national identity. For many Ugandans, a sense of pride and belonging is derived from tribal identity. On the other hand, long-term stability and peace will only be achieved when that such identities are widely perceived to be of little significance in the enjoyment of the civil, political, social, and economic rights derived from being a citizen of the state of Uganda.

Buganda

The politics of identity has three main dimensions in Uganda today. One of these is the perception that Buganda has always been somehow special, and that amongst the constituent elements of modern Uganda it should be the first amongst equals.This issue has dogged politics in Uganda since the prospect of independence in the mid-1950s. At an

▲ The Monitor and New Vision are the daily newspapers sold nationwide in Uganda. Both papers are able to express views and allegations that are critical of the government.

early stage in its struggle, the NRM made a commitment to correct historical wrongs, and to do so in a way that would promote, rather than fracture, national unity. Monarchists and other traditional leaders may have understood this commitment to mean the restoration of a state of Buganda, with all of its pre-1966 powers. Instead, however, the NRM opted to restore the kingdoms as expressions of cultural identity, but not as political or economic entities. In 1993 the Kabaka, who had returned from exile in 1986, was crowned, and his property and the symbols of his power were returned. Kingdoms were also restored in Busoga, Toro, and Bunyoro, as part of a concerted approach to balance the acknowledgement of group identities without compromising loyalty and obedience to the state of Uganda.

The federalist inclinations that may have been encouraged by the Kabaka's restoration were rejected, in a debate that was long, hard, and which went right up to the wire, in the constitutional settlement of 1995. It is too soon to know whether the Baganda have accepted this settlement as the best way of preserving their cultural identity, at the same time as confirming Buganda's status as being equal with other parts of the country.

The western factor

The second dimension of the politics of identity is a consequence of the increasingly evident economic and social inequalities between different parts of the country. The core of the argument is that the NRM stands guilty of the very wrong it was set up to eliminate – sectarianism. In a recent article in the *New Vision,* the daily paper that is closest to the government, a critic observed that 'milk and honey flow predominantly in the homeland of the rulers, western Uganda.' It is testimony to the freedom of speech and to the vitality of Uganda's media that these kinds of allegations are openly aired.

The view that people from the west of Uganda are increasingly dominating the political, military, and commercial life of the country is very widely held. Although numerous individuals within the government, civil service, and other arenas of public life, retain fully deserved reputations for integrity, critics can quote many examples of the alleged improper use of office or information by public officials. The values that once made the NRM distinctive and refreshing are in danger of being sullied by the politics of parochialism and the economics of personal gain.

From the Movement to movements

The third dimension of the politics of identity in Uganda has been the emergence of social movements and interest groups. There has been a mushrooming of these groups in the last 15 years, with the result that there are now thousands of small, community-based groups as well as larger NGOs in Uganda. Some of these groups have developed into well-defined and influential social movements, such as the disability movement or the women's movement, which are both formally incorporated into the political system. These movements have grown in size, visibility, and organising capacity, and have engaged effectively in the political process. They have not been 'co-opted' into the Movement, but have retained their independence of identity and organisation. For the first time in Uganda's post-independence history, alternative forms of social organisation that are not based on sectarian divisions are being forged. Together with an independent and courageous media, these organisations are testimony to the emergence of an active, questioning citizenship, challenging the notion that politics is the preserve of the few.

Changing attitudes to disability

Julius Mayanja is a doctor and a lecturer at Mbarara Medical School. He is also a member of the LC5, the district council, elected on the basis of a provision in the constitution that says that there should be two disabled representatives on each LC.

'In general, attitudes, public perceptions of disability, have changed rapidly. People see our abilities rather than simply our weaknesses or inabilities. Legislation did play a part in raising the profile of these issues, but the development of associations for particular disabilities was vital to make those disabilities visible. Epilepsy,

▼ Julius Mubangizi, who has been elected as a sub-county councillor. Uganda's high-profile disabled movement has worked to transform attitudes to disability and to promote the inclusion of disabled people in all areas of society and politics.

Geoff Sayer

▲ Bruno has cerebral palsy. His parents, Gertrude and Gabriel Kamateme, explained how disabled groups and government advice have helped them to enable Bruno to make huge progress. Soon, Bruno will be attending school for the first time.

Geoff Sayer

for example, affects many thousands in this district alone, but it was hardly considered; it was not an issue, not on the government's agenda nor the public's. No-one realised how common it was. It came to light when the associations counted the numbers affected in the sub-counties. [They found] thousands of cases of epilepsy. Now we have been able to budget more funds for these drugs, drugs that were hardly available before, because the numbers convinced everyone.'

Julius Mubangizi is a councillor at the LC3 level. He suffers from albinism, a condition by which the pigmentation process that confers skin colour is impaired. The impairment means that Julius appears white. It also damages his sight and threatens the onset of skin cancers at an early age. It is a form of disability that tends to provoke prejudice rather than sympathy.

'I first came to understand that I was different when I started school. I was used to the families in our neighbourhood, and they were used to me [but at school] other children despised me – they called me names and abused me. I had a hat that I wore to school [to protect his skin against the sun] and the others would take it off me and throw it in the mud. They beat me to see if I would cry like them, if I would bleed. After some time the teachers became aware of the problem and starting protecting me. But it was very harsh in those early years.'

After leaving secondary school, Julius worked as a telephone operator but was made redundant with the introduction of new technology in 1993. Three years later, in 1996, he became a member of a local group of people with disabilities.

'We have organisations which unite us as disabled people, and I think that has helped us all. We have a common struggle, and we are all aware of what we want to achieve. This has been the great change that I have seen in my lifetime.

'Before I found out about disabled organisations, I didn't even know much about other disabled people. I didn't even know much about myself. First you have to believe in yourself, and that's what the group has helped me to do, to gain confidence in myself. Six or seven years ago I could not have addressed a crowd, or even a small group. Now I can do it. I used to stay at home and depend on the family. I didn't help myself. Now I hire land and work on it. I look for ways to make an income. I'm not a dependant. I can help support the younger children.

'The disabled movement and the changes it has brought have helped me to participate in society, and now even to participate in the country's government. We have our representatives, even a minister. This has give us, as disabled people, a higher profile; it has brought us more into contact with people at all levels of society and government, and shown that we can do things for ourselves. We have learned that we have abilities, and society, seeing this, has also learned that we have a place, a role to play, just as they do. They can see that we are not so different after all.'

Conclusion:
an end to conflict

Looking back on their daily lives over the last 40 years or so, the majority of Uganda's citizens will reflect on the turbulence of the times they have lived through. In some respects, there has been little change in the patterns of daily life for millions of Ugandans. People continue to cultivate the land by hand, or to herd their animals in ways that have barely altered since Uganda was created a hundred years ago. They continue to provide for their own subsistence, with relatively little contact with external markets. This sense of continuity was captured by Lorochom, the Karimojong elder, who explained, 'Governments change and the weather changes... but we continue herding our animals.'

There have been some positive changes, however. The mismanagement of Uganda's economy under the regimes of Idi Amin and Obote II left Uganda amongst the poorest countries in the world. Improved management of the national economy has been one of the great achievements of the NRM and, provided that aid flows do not significantly diminish, Ugandans can reasonably look forward to continued economic growth, better public services, and further investments in essential infrastructure.

▲ *Margaret Muhindo in her kitchen garden. In a good year, she will be able to sell surplus vegetables for cash. In a bad year, she and her family will scrape by on the food they grow.*

Nonetheless, turbulence has been the defining feature of the age, and it is in the political realm that turbulence has been profoundly destructive. Instead of protecting the lives and property of its citizens, the state in one form or other has been responsible for the murder, torture, harassment, displacement, and impoverishment of its people.

Wherever they live, Ugandans have experienced the consequences of the misuse of political power. They have seen the consequences of human rights abuses and killings. They have suffered the depredations of economic collapse. They have recognised the direct relationship between peace and security, and economic and social development. There is an overwhelming desire for peace, justice, and equal opportunities for all Ugandans.

But the spectre of sectarianism still haunts the country. When Uganda became independent, it inherited divisions so deep that intense political struggle was inevitable. These divisions have been the cause of continuous internal conflict. The current concentration of political, economic, and military power in southern and western areas of the country has left other areas feeling excluded and neglected.

The government has rightly won plaudits for the adoption of a comprehensive, poverty-focused development strategy which has the potential to make a huge difference to the lives of millions of Ugandans. However, policies to increase the incomes of the poor and to provide better public services will have no impact in the parts of the country where conflict and insecurity are ongoing. In these districts, the productive base of the economy has been wrecked because people have limited access to land or their animals have been stolen. Market systems fail, and schools and health centres have been closed or barely function.

The young girl, forced to flee her home, who lies on the concrete veranda of the hospital in Kitgum trying to read her schoolbooks in the feeble light, will have little chance to benefit from the education revolution. There is a danger that even progressive policies like the introduction of universal primary education will bring benefits to some Ugandans and not others. If this happens these policies could contribute to increasing inequalities in Uganda, rather than fulfilling their potential to make a positive contribution to nation building.

Nationhood will be achieved, and sectarianism finally laid to rest, only if the government takes a determined political initiative to end the conflict in the north, and to prevent the conflict in its western border areas deteriorating into a similar stalemate in which the primary losers are displaced civilian populations. An end to conflict would constitute the single most important contribution to nation building. The effectiveness of the political system that has been so carefully crafted in the last 15 years will ultimately be judged by its ability to create a nation at peace with itself, and capable of delivering economic and social progress for all of its citizens.

Geoff Sayer

▲ *A rainy night for those sleeping outside at Kitgum Mission Hospital, northern Uganda. Every night, hundreds of families come here from their villages to sleep in safety, out of reach of violent rebels.*

▼ *Reaching for the sky. Girls from Nakawanga Primary School in Rakai district play netball.*

Geoff Sayer

Facts and figures

Geoff Sayer

Adult literacy
64 per cent
(female: 53 per cent)

Access to electricity
3-5 per cent of population

Gross domestic product (GDP)
US$ 6.6 billion total;
US$ 310 per capita

Annual GDP growth rate
6 per cent (2000 estimate)

External debt
US $3.3 billion
(2000 estimate)

Land area
241,000 km²

Population
22.21 million (official estimate, 2000)
13 per cent urban; 87 per cent rural

Average life expectancy
women: 40.4 years; men: 38.9 years

Under-five mortality rate
137 deaths per 1000 live births

Ratio of doctors to patients
1: 25,000

Cases of HIV infection
1.9 million (estimated)

Access to safe water
46 per cent

Primary school completion
49 per cent of boys; 25 per cent of girls

Secondary school enrolment
13 per cent (female: 7 per cent)

Currency
New Ugandan Shilling;
average exchange rate:
NUSh 1640 = US$1.00 (2000 estimate)

Principal exports
Coffee (55 per cent of total exports);
fish (7.4 per cent); tea (5.3 per cent);
tobacco (4.2 per cent); cotton (1.4 per cent);
cut flowers (1.4 per cent)

Human Development Index ranking
158

(Sources:
UNDP: *Human Development Report 1999*;
Economist Intelligence Unit:
Uganda: *Country Profile 1999-2000* and
Uganda: *Country Report 2001*)

Dates and events

c1500 AD Establishment of kingdoms in southern and western Uganda.

1840-50 Arab traders begin to establish trading links in Buganda.

1870s The first Christian missionaries arrive in Buganda.

1884 British domination of Uganda (as part of British East Africa) is agreed at the Berlin Conference.

1894 Britain declares the Uganda protectorate.

1900 The Buganda Agreement is signed.

1900-20 The immigration of craftsmen and traders from the Indian sub-continent is encouraged as a way of increasing commercial capacity.

1945-50 Anti-colonial resistance begins to emerge in different forms.

1962 Uganda gains independence.

1966 Milton Obote suspends the 1962 Ugandan constitution and declares himself Executive President. The Baganda Parliament rejects the interim constitution. The army crushes Buganda's opposition.

1967 A new constitution is approved and the kingdoms are abolished.

1969 Political parties are banned.

1971 Idi Amin overthrows President Obote.

1972 The economic war is declared, and Ugandan Asians are given three months to leave. The Chief Justice is murdered.

Geoff Sayer

Fiona O'Mahoney

1986 The National Resistance Army (NRA) takes control of Kampala and Yoweri Museveni becomes President. War continues in the north and east against the Holy Spirit Movement and other rebel groups.

1987 The NRA reaches agreement with the IMF and adopts an economic reform package. The Holy Spirit Movement dissolves.

1977 Pastoral letter from the bishops of the Church of Uganda protesting against harassment and atrocities. Archbishop Luwum is murdered. The East Africa Community collapses.

1978 Uganda invades Tanzania. War begins.

1979 The Tanzanian army and Ugandan opposition groups take the war into Uganda. Amin flees, and Yusuf Lule is sworn in as President. Lule is soon replaced as President by Godfrey Binaisa.

1980 Binaisa is overthrown by the Military Commission headed by Paulo Muwanga. Obote returns to Uganda. Elections are held, and Milton Obote becomes President again.

1981 Yoweri Museveni leads guerrilla attack on military training school, signalling the start of the 'bush war'. Obote reaches agreement with the IMF and foreign backers.

1982 Massive expulsion of Banyarwanda from various parts of west and central Uganda.

1984 First AIDS cases reported. Agreement with the IMF breaks down amidst increasing internal insecurity and economic turmoil.

1985 Milton Obote is overthrown.

1989 Countrywide Resistance Council elections held, leading to an expanded National Resistance Council.

1991 Major military operation to counter insurgency forces in northern Uganda.

1993 The National Resistance Council restores the institution of traditional rulers, abolished under the 1967 constitution. The first private radio station in Uganda starts broadcasting.

1995 The Lord's Resistance Army begins major attacks in the north. A new constitution is appoved by the Constituent Assembly.

1996 President Museveni retains his position as President of the Republic of Uganda in the first direct presidential elections. He announces free primary education for four children from each family.

1997 Poverty eradication designated as the key policy objective of government.

2000 The Referendum on the Political System confirms support for the retention of a Movement, not a multi-party, system.

2001 Presidential elections – Museveni is re-elected.

Sources and further reading

Politics and economics

Holger Bernt Hansen and Michael Twaddle (eds.):
Uganda Now (1988);
Changing Uganda (1991);
From Chaos to Order (1995);
Developing Uganda (1998);
all Oxford: James Currey

Arne Bigsten and Steve Kayizzi-Mugerwa (1999),
*Crisis, Adjustment and Growth in Uganda:
A Study of Adaptation in an African Economy*,
London: Palgrave

Mahmood Mamdani (1999), *Politics and Class
Formation in Uganda,* Kampala: Fountain
Publishers

Yoweri Museveni (1997), *Sowing the Mustard
Seed*, London: Palgrave

Monitor (newspaper),
http://www.monitor.co.ug

New Vision (newspaper),
http//www.newvision.co.ug

History

Giles Foden (1999), *The Last King of Scotland,*
London: Faber and Faber

Thomas P Ofcansky (1996), *Uganda: Tarnished
Pearl of Africa,* Boulder CO: Westview Press

HIV/AIDS

Janey Hampton (1990), *Living Positively with
AIDS: The AIDS Support Organisation,*
Uganda: Action Aid/AMREF/World in Need

Noerine Kaleeba, Joyce Namulondo Kadowe,
Daniel Kalinaki, and Glen Williams (2000),
Open Secret, Uganda: Action Aid

http://www.swiftuganda.com/~strtalk/

http://www.newafrica.com/uganda/

http://www.hivinsite.ucsf.edu/

Conflict

Amnesty International (1997), Breaking God's
Commands: The Destruction of Childhood
by the LRA, London: Amnesty International

Amnesty International (1999),
*Protecting Human Rights in the
Northern War Zone*, London:
Amnesty International

Human Rights Watch (1997), *The
Scars of Death: Children Abducted
by the LRA in Uganda*, New York:
Human Rights Watch

Robert Gersony (1997), *The
Anguish of Northern Uganda:
Results of a Field-Based Assessment
of the Civil Conflicts in Northern
Uganda*, Washington DC: USAID

Geoff Sayer

Acknowledgements

The idea of producing a Country Profile on Uganda has been kept alive for years by Catherine Robinson of the Publications Team in Oxfam. Her determination has finally been rewarded! Thanks are due first and foremost to individual Ugandans who were consistently willing to answer questions and describe the reality of their lives to enquiring outsiders.

Some of these individuals are mentioned by name in this book, some are not – but to all of them I express my most sincere gratitude. Some of those individuals have even had to endure two or three interviews spread over several years – and for their patience and tolerance particular thanks are due.

Jenny Matthews

I would like to thank all Oxfam staff in Kampala, Kitgum, and Karamoja,who gave us all the time, support, and practical assistance we needed. It was a real pleasure to work in such a positive atmosphere.

In compiling the information for this book we benefited from the generosity of numerous organisations and individuals. In particular I would like to acknowledge the collaborative spirit of staff in Action Aid who were extremely generous with access to information derived from their work on HIV/AIDS in Uganda. Action Aid's work is itself described at length in the book *Open Secret*. Special mention should also be made of the staff of the Lutheran World Federation's Karamoja Agro-Pastoral Development Programme who were extremely generous with their time and access to materials. The section on insecurity in Karamoja draws extensively from their work.

This book has been improved considerably by the thoughtful, and sometimes extensive, comments and advice from several readers: Judy Adoko, Izzy Birch, Johnson Byamukama, Justus Mugaju, Leonard Okello, Dennis Pain, Nick Stockton, Kennedy Tumutegyereize, Dereje Wordofa. I would particularly like to thank the editor, Kate Kilpatrick, for her perseverance, tolerance, and encouragement.

I have a special debt of gratitude to my long time colleague, Geoff Sayer. His commitment and energy are legendary and I have benefited enormously from working with him. He took almost all the photographs in this book, and gathered much of the interview material.

I have a second special debt of gratitude to Debbie Mander, who typed up dozens of interviews as well as numerous drafts of this book. Her reliability is absolute and I would never have been able to meet the deadlines without her support and humour.

Ian Leggett

Oxfam in Uganda

Geoff Sayer

Oxfam GB works to relieve poverty, suffering, and distress in Ugandan communities through long term development and humanitarian response and preparedness. Oxfam has worked in Uganda since 1963.

Uganda faces the challenge of worsening poverty levels arising from armed conflict among rebel movements in the west and north of the country, and the Karimojong conflict in the northeast. Drought and famine frequently affect the Karamoja region. In these areas, Oxfam provides humanitarian assistance, works to ensure food and livelihood security, and supports peace-building in communities torn apart by conflict.

In Kitgum district, Oxfam provides direct humanitarian assistance to internally displaced people and is implementing a livelihood security programme. In the eastern part of the district, Oxfam's livelihood protection programme provides job opportunities for people who have lost their land or cattle as a result of the pastoral crisis. In Kabarole, Kasese, and Bundibugyo districts, Oxfam promotes emergency public health and hygiene. In Kotido district, Oxfam works with pastoral communities to promote secure livelihoods, peace-building, and humanitarian monitoring.

Oxfam works with the Ugandan government and with other NGOs to improve communities' abilities to prepare for and cope with disaster situations. To prevent crises in communities vulnerable to famine, Oxfam is engaged in nutrition monitoring and capacity-building for relief agencies. Oxfam supports the monitoring and preparedness of district authorities in Kitgum to contain the spread of the deadly Ebola virus.

Oxfam recognises that to relieve poverty and distress in Uganda, all Ugandans must have an effective voice in influencing the policy decisions affecting their lives. Oxfam in Uganda supports groups working to influence policy on poverty issues such as land ownership, debt relief, corruption, accountability, women's empowerment, and representation for vulnerable and marginalised people. The Ugandan Participatory Poverty Assessment Process gives some of Uganda's poorest communities an opportunity to voice their views, concerns, and demands on issues like these. Oxfam has been able to use this process to influence government policy to ensure increased accountability, increased spending on social services, and favourable policies for vulnerable people. Oxfam in Uganda is also directly participating in the formulation of the government's National Poverty Eradication Plan.

Index